D1599772

BY ART THOMAS

KAINOS PUBLISHING

An imprint of:
SUPERNATURAL TRUTH PRODUCTIONS, LLC
Practical Training for Spirit-Filled Living
www.SupernaturalTruth.com

ISBN: 978-0-9988171-8-7

TABLE OF CONTENTS

INTRODUCTION:

A NOTE TO THE READER:

I assume you're reading this book because you just became a Christian.

Welcome to your new life!

This book is written especially for you as a new follower of Jesus. It's not everything you will ever need to know, and it probably won't answer all your questions. You have your whole life ahead of you to discover the deep wonders of God and his love for you. This book simply offers the foundational principles that will help you thrive in your walk with God.

Jesus told his followers they needed to humble themselves and become like little children.[1] He said that his supernatural, heavenly "kingdom" belonged to such people.[2] Because of this, I believe the Christian life is *not* complicated.

Yes, there are incredible, deep truths to discover. You can study the Bible your whole life yet still have more to learn. You can know Jesus for decades yet feel as if you've barely scratched the surface of all there is to enjoy of him. But when it comes to application—to actually living the Christian life— it's so easy, a child could do it.

This book contains stories from the Bible, from my life, and from the lives of people close to me. Along the way, I'll share some of my struggles and wins. And I trust that by the

---

[1] See Matthew 18:2–3.
[2] See Matthew 19:14.

end, you'll find yourself encouraged and ready to live for Jesus throughout the rest of your life.

I'll teach you how to read the Bible, how to pray, and how to share your faith with others. We'll talk about the exciting new life that lays ahead of you, God's powerful presence that helps you in life, and the new identity you now have in Jesus.

From now on, everything is going to be different, and I know it will be different for the better.

God loves you more than you could possibly imagine, and I pray he will make that love known to you as you read. I pray your heart is stirred with every word on every page. I pray that you encounter God's powerful presence even now.

He is with you.

He lives in you.

You are a child of God.

Welcome to my family,

[signature: Art Thomas]

Art Thomas
Pastor / Leadership Director
Roots Church, AG
www.RootsAG.org

CHAPTER 1:

YOUR NEW LIFE

*I have been crucified with Christ and I no longer live, but
Christ lives in me. The life I now live in the body, I live by faith in
the Son of God, who loved me and gave himself for me.*

—GALATIANS 2:20

Christianity is the most thrilling, difficult, fun, risky,
comforting, scary, fulfilling, and life-transforming lifestyle in
existence. It's full of both blessings and challenges. You'll
encounter mountaintops so high you'll think you're already in
heaven and valleys so low you might wonder if you made the
right choice.

In October 2011, I took my first trip to a remote African
village in Uganda called Wanenga. There, I lived for
seventeen days with a pastor named Paul, his wife Helen, their
five children, an elderly man they adopted off the streets
named John, and sixteen orphans. Their entire house was
about the size of my living room and kitchen, and they gave
me their best room to sleep in. They overwhelmed me with
love and kindness, almost embarrassing me with their
generosity and hospitality.

Paul grew up believing in another religion. At the time,
his name was Habib. As a teenager, one of his friends told him
that he should come to the Christian church one week because
"the women there do not wear head-coverings." Naturally,
Habib went to church, excited to see for himself.

7

ROOTED

At the church meeting, the preacher invited people to abandon their "sinful lifestyles" that dishonored God and kept them from knowing him. He told those who wanted to surrender their lives to Jesus to come to the front of the church and receive prayer for their salvation. Habib felt as though a hand grabbed the back of his shirt, lifted him off the bench, and carried him to the front of the church. But when he looked, no one had touched him!

He suddenly had a vision of light shining out of heaven and covering him. He received God's forgiveness that day, asked the Holy Spirit to make a home in his heart, and instantly felt like a brand-new person.

But his family was not so happy. By leaving their traditional beliefs, Habib had brought shame on them and disgraced his ancestors. His own parents disowned him. His former family chased him away from home, cursing him and trying to kill him. Habib became an orphan and was taken in by a pastor who had pity on him.

Habib soon changed his name to Paul Basuule. "Basuule" means "garbage" or "throwaway." He says, "When I became a Christian, my family threw me away like trash, but Jesus saw my value and picked me up!"

In time, Paul became a pastor and soon felt God was asking him to move out to the village of Wanenga to start a church. When he arrived, the town was full of witchdoctors and drunkards. He built a small mud hut there with a grass-thatched roof. As soon as he could, he began telling people about Jesus.

And they beat him.

Paul suffered greatly. But little by little, he introduced the villagers to Jesus and began to teach them on Sunday in a small shed made from sticks and banana leaves.

Sometimes, Paul was attacked for preaching about Jesus, but God always spared his life. Once, a group of men came with clubs from a nearby village where he had gone to preach. They wanted to kill him. Paul watched through the open door of his hut as the crowd of men marched past along the path, not knowing where he lived. About ten minutes later, Paul watched the same men running in the opposite direction.

He later learned that the men entered the village square and demanded that the people bring out the pastor. But the drunkards who had previously been so mean to Paul now saw the good he was doing. And even though they weren't ready to give up their drunkenness and follow Jesus, they said to the men with the sticks, "You leave our pastor alone!" And then the drunken men chased the men with sticks straight out of the village.

Today as I write, Paul and I have planted twelve churches in remote villages, including a couple on an island in Lake Victoria. We've built an orphanage and school that educates about five hundred children and houses about fifty.

Many times, Paul has taken me to remote villages to introduce people to Jesus. We have seen amazing miracles as Christians prayed for each other—things like those you read about in the Bible. People who were blind can now see. People who were deaf can now hear. Paralyzed legs can now walk. Tumors have disappeared, skin conditions have cleared up, and all manner of sicknesses have been miraculously cured as people ministered to each other "in the name of Jesus."

But at the same time, we know that the message of Jesus will also bring tremendous challenges to some people. Some will be chased away from home. Some may be beaten or even killed. In their world, giving one's life to Jesus could cost everything.

So when I tell people about Jesus and as Paul translates for me, I often ask him to share his story. And when I invite people to know Jesus, I often say, "I cannot promise you that if you give your life to Jesus, everything in your life will be wonderful. What I *can* promise you is that Jesus is worth any cost."

And he is.

Cost and Reward

Chances are, you don't live in a place like the remote villages of eastern Uganda. Chances are, your life isn't in danger because of your decision to follow Jesus. But the cost of following Jesus is still the same: *everything.*

Suppose a man is walking through a field and stumbles upon a half-buried treasure. He investigates further and realizes there is an entire cave filled with gold and precious artifacts.

He knows the field doesn't belong to him, so taking the treasure would be stealing, and he would surely be caught trying to haul away all the loot. But the man has an idea: If I buy the field, then the treasure in it would belong to me!

He quickly hides the treasure so the current owner doesn't see it. He scurries home to run the numbers and quickly realizes he will need to sell everything he owns in order to afford the field.

But he knows the treasure in that field will be worth more than his wildest dreams!

What would you do?

I didn't make up this story. It's based on one Jesus told.[1] Following Jesus costs us our entire lives, but the treasure we find in following him is worth so much more.

I often tell people that following Jesus is like signing your name to the bottom of a blank contract, handing it to Jesus, and saying, "You fill in the details. I trust you. I don't care what it costs me. You're worth any price. I'm surrendering my ideas about morality, my beliefs about who I am, and my expectations for the future. And I now want to learn your definition of morality, your declaration of who I am, and your plans for my eternity. I believe that whatever you have for me is better than any other option."

---

[1] See Matthew 13:44.

You don't literally have to sell all your possessions to follow Jesus, but you do have to believe that Jesus is King—that everything you own technically belongs to him now. As generosity wells up in your heart, you may find yourself wanting to give away belongings to people in need. But even if you continue to enjoy what you have, you will find that you do so with a sense of gratitude, knowing that your Father in heaven provided all of it.

I have preached in about twenty different countries—some in which Christianity is illegal and some where the local people hate and persecute Christians. I have friends whose property has been stolen. I know others whose homes have been burned down. I personally know people who have been beaten for daring to follow Jesus. These friends of mine have literally decided that Jesus is worth dying for. But even in a safe country like the one in which I live, the doorway to new life looks like a cross.

Time to Die

I grew up in a Christian home with wonderful parents. But even the best parents in the world can't protect their children from everything. When I was about seven or eight years old, some older boys in my neighborhood sexually abused me. And I regret to say that I quickly went from "victim" to "this is the game we play." Soon, a friend down the street showed me a pornographic magazine that he found under his stepdad's bed. I was hooked.

In middle school, when my family finally connected our home PC to the internet, I kept myself awake late at night when I knew my parents were sleeping and wouldn't hear the dial-up modem screeching (now you have an idea how old I am!) just so I could look at images I shouldn't.

I was addicted, depressed, and filled with rage. I was an emotional and spiritual mess.

But there was another problem: I *really* loved Jesus. I didn't want to live this way. But no matter how hard I tried to do the right thing, I kept messing up again and again.

I struggled for years, wishing I could be free. I wish I could share my entire story with you here, but for now I'll simply say that at the age of sixteen, I discovered something in the Bible that transformed my life.[2]

One of the people God empowered to write the Bible was a man named Paul. (My friend in Uganda named himself after this biblical hero.) Paul wrote a letter to a church in a region called Galatia (now part of Turkey). In that letter, he wrote, "I have been crucified with Christ and I no longer live, but Christ lives in me. The life I now live in the body, I live by faith in the Son of God, who loved me and gave himself for me."[3]

What was Paul talking about?

Well, we know Jesus was crucified. He was unfairly arrested, brutally beaten, viciously whipped, and nailed to a wooden cross where he hung naked, bleeding, and suffocating for all to see. While there, he forgave the people killing him, welcomed a thief into his kingdom, and cried out to his Father in heaven. After six hours of agony, he entrusted his spirit into Father God's hands, and he died.

We also know that he was wrapped in grave clothes, sealed in a tomb, and on the morning of the third day after his death, he miraculously came back to life.

But what I don't see anywhere in that story is Paul. How can Paul say he was crucified with Christ? And how can he say that he no longer lives? If he's dead, how did he even write those words?

---

[2] To hear my entire story of how God transformed my life, search YouTube.com for a video titled "Identity, Authority, and Forgiveness - Art Thomas Ministries."
[3] Galatians 2:20.

This short passage of Scripture contains a powerful truth. Your past no longer defines how you live or the future that awaits you. You don't have to be ruled by the traumas you've experienced. You're no longer defined by whatever terrible things anyone has ever said about you or done to you. And you're no longer identified by any sinful activity, behavior, or habit from your past. The person you once were is now dead.

Paul wrote another letter to a group of Christians in a Greek city called Corinth. There he said, "Therefore, if anyone is in Christ, the new creation has come: The old has gone, the new is here!"[4] By surrendering your life to Jesus, you have become a completely different person. The lost, sinful person you once were is considered dead. God no longer sees your past attached to you.

And as Paul said to the Galatians, the life we *now* live is "by faith." That means the only way we can live differently than we used to is if we trust God to change our very nature and express his own love and power through us.

When I saw all this at the age of sixteen, I realized my problem. Time after time, I would sin with rage, lust, bitterness, and more. This would continue until I was so miserable, I couldn't take it anymore. I would finally crawl back to Jesus and ask for forgiveness, and he would graciously set me free. I would feel clean and new.

But as soon as those feelings wore off, I would go right back to my old life and do the same things all over again.

I finally realized that I had come to Jesus over and over again to be forgiven, but I had never come to him to die.

Peter, one of Jesus's followers, wrote that Jesus took all our sins into his physical body on the cross so that we could receive God's righteous perfection and live new lives.[5] Along those lines, Paul went so far as to say that Jesus actually

---

[4] 2 Corinthians 5:17.
[5] See 1 Peter 2:24.

ROO⊤ED

"became sin" on the cross so that we could "become the righteousness of God."[6] In other words, when Jesus died, sin died.

My sin died.

Your sin died.

And when Jesus came out of the grave, all that sin stayed dead. Jesus defeated it for us so that we could live free. Just as Jesus took all our sin into himself on the cross, he now puts all his goodness and perfection into us. He became sin, and now we who believe in him have become righteousness.[7]

But the good news doesn't stop there. Paul also wrote to a church in Rome, saying:

> Now if we died with Christ, we believe that we will also live with him. For we know that since Christ was raised from the dead, he cannot die again; death no longer has mastery over him. The death he died, he died to sin once for all; but the life he lives, he lives to God.
>
> In the same way, count yourselves dead to sin but alive to God in Christ Jesus.[8]

Paul is basically commanding his readers to think of themselves as though the same thing that happened to Jesus happened to us—that we were once the embodiment of sin, but we have died to it and are now raised up to new life. We are completely free from sin.

Thinking Differently

When I discovered that I could consider my old life dead and live in real freedom, everything started to change. I forgave those older boys in my neighborhood for abusing me.

---

[6] See 2 Corinthians 5:21.
[7] "Righteousness" is a word that basically means perfection, implying that justice has prevailed to set things right.
[8] Romans 6:8–11.

I forgave my friend for introducing me to pornography. I forgave my parents for any shortcomings. I forgave various pastors for not showing me this truth sooner. And although he did nothing wrong, I even forgave God, releasing all the anger I had bottled up against him for "letting so many bad things happen to me."

I learned that God didn't cause all the tragedies and traumas. If God wanted those horrible things to happen to me, then he wouldn't have sent his Son, Jesus, to conquer evil on the cross. God didn't hurt me; sin hurt me. And Jesus came to obliterate sin.

I began to think differently.

We Christians use a certain Bible word, but not everyone knows what it means: *repent*. In the original Greek language, which was used to write the latter part of the Bible, this word means to "change one's mind."[9] To "repent" implies turning around and going in a different direction, and we do this first in the way we think.

A lot of people use the word "repent" in reference to behavior: "change the way you act." But a real, lasting change of behavior starts with the way you think.

Suppose you are in a building with some friends, and a stranger bursts through the door, announcing, "Everyone scream and run outside!" How likely are you to comply?

Now suppose someone else bursts in and shouts, "This building is on fire!" Chances are, anyone who believes the messenger is going to jump up, scream, and run out of the building.

When someone told the people how to behave, no one saw the point. But when someone told the people what to

---

[9] "μετανοέω." Walter Bauer, ed. Frederick W. Danker, *A Greek-English Lexicon of the New Testament and Other Early Christian Literature, Third Edition*, trans. William F. Arndt and F. Wilbur Gingrich (Chicago: University of Chicago Press, 2000), 640.

believe, those who embraced the new thought immediately behaved accordingly. Changed behavior is the natural response to changed belief.

All my life, I had been trying to change the way I behaved. I desperately wanted to stop. But it wasn't until I considered myself dead and truly believed that Jesus lives in me that my lifestyle finally started to change.

It was admittedly a process. The most intense part took about five years, but in many ways, I'm still in process. Little by little, day by day, God's Holy Spirit is making me more and more like Jesus in my actions, words, and attitudes. He's teaching me to trust and to love.

Jesus is transforming us into the sort of people who change the world—people like himself.

Your New Position

John, one of Jesus's first followers, wrote a powerful statement, declaring, "This is how love is made complete among us so that we will have confidence on the day of judgment: In this world we are like Jesus."[10]

A day of judgment is coming for everyone who has ever lived. The judge is God himself, and his verdict will be final. There are no appeals courts in eternity. It can be terrifying if you focus on it too much, but it's a reality.

But John said we can have confidence on that day. Why? Because we're like Jesus.

I don't believe John is saying that unless your life looks perfectly like Jesus right now that you can't be confident about how you'll fare in the judgment. Rather, I believe that John is pointing to a greater reality. We are new creations because of Jesus. God's Holy Spirit lives inside us, expressing God's love and nature through our actions, words, and attitudes as we continue to trust him. And every time Jesus expresses his love,

---

[10] 1 John 4:17.

goodness, and righteousness through us, we can celebrate the fact that our salvation is certain.

"In this world, we are like Jesus." What a wild proposition. Since John's words were originally written in Greek, many different scholars have carefully translated them into English throughout the centuries. Sometimes different translators use varied words to express different nuances, even though the meaning remains the same. One old translation, called the New King James Version, says, "As He is, so are we in this world."[11] We're not simply following some ancient example of what Jesus used to be like. We are expressing the living Jesus as he is right now—alive, victorious, powerful, amazing, and seated on a throne.

In many countries today, we don't really understand the significance of being seated on a throne. Many of us think more in terms of democracy. But at the time the Bible was written, brutal empires rose and fell. Kings and rulers lorded over people. Whoever sat on the throne was the supreme authority in that realm.[12]

There are thrones in heaven. Father God sits in the highest position. And at the Father's right hand—at the next highest place of authority—sits Jesus.

Check out what Paul wrote about the victorious place Jesus holds in heaven: "Therefore God exalted him to the highest place and gave him the name that is above every name, that at the name of Jesus every knee should bow, in heaven and on earth and under the earth, and every tongue acknowledge that Jesus Christ is Lord, to the glory of God the Father."[13]

---

[11] 1 John 4:17 (NKJV).
[12] It's worth saying, though, that the way God rules from his throne is different and better than any earthly king. Jesus revealed the unthinkable: a king who serves his people. (See Luke 12:37.)
[13] Philippians 2:9–11.

ROOTED

The throne on which Jesus sits, next to Father God, is the highest place anyone but Father God could hold. This is the risen, victorious Jesus who expresses himself through us by the power of the Holy Spirit. Paul went so far as to say, "And God raised us up with Christ and seated us with him in the heavenly realms in Christ Jesus."[14]

Do you see it? When we entrust our lives to Jesus, everything changes. We consider our old lives dead, and as such, we die with him. Then, the same Holy Spirit of God who raised Jesus from the dead comes to live inside us.[15] We become new creations—people who never existed before. Then he gives us his own authority—not so that we can lord over people like an evil emperor but so that our service to people is both empowered and meaningful. Jesus begins to express his love and goodness through us so that when people encounter us, they encounter him.

That's the sort of lifestyle that's worth giving up everything for. It's why my Ugandan friend Paul would be willing to abandon the security of his family and the religion of his ancestors to serve Jesus in a rural village where people want him dead. It's why my friends around the world have joyfully accepted persecution and threats. It's why I've been willing to share Jesus with armed gangs in Rio de Janeiro, Brazil, and Port-au-Prince, Haiti. It's why I have shared Jesus in places where I could be imprisoned, attacked, or deported.

It's why someone shared Jesus with you.

This is what it looks like to follow Jesus, and it's worth any cost.

Welcome to the adventure of a lifetime.

Welcome to your new life.

---

[14] Ephesians 2:6.
[15] See Romans 8:11.

CHAPTER 2

FOLLOWING JESUS

*As Jesus was walking beside the Sea of Galilee, he saw
two brothers, Simon called Peter and his brother Andrew.
They were casting a net into the lake, for they were fishermen.
"Come, follow me," Jesus said, "and I will send you out to
fish for people." At once they left their nets and followed him.*

—MATTHEW 4:18–20

In today's world, when someone says they "follow" someone, they might mean that they've opted in to seeing social media posts from that person. But in the time of Jesus, to follow someone meant to dedicate yourself to learning from that person and patterning your life after them.

Jesus offered a small group of fishermen an incredible opportunity. He was preaching to a crowd by the side of a lake. The people were pressing in, so Jesus hopped onto a small, flat fishing boat near the shore and asked its owner to push out a little into the water.

The boat's owner—a fisherman named Simon—was weary from a fruitless night of fishing. He probably just wanted to wash his nets and go home. But this teacher seemed like an important figure, so Simon obliged.

Jesus sat down in the boat and preached to the crowd that stood along the shore, the water carrying his voice so all could hear.

ROOTED

When he was done teaching, Jesus turned to Simon and said, "Move out into deep water and let down your nets for a catch."

Simon vented his frustration about fishing all night without results. Then he added, "But because you say so, I will let down the nets."

Simon and his small fishing crew rowed out a bit and dropped their nets unceremoniously into the sea, not likely expecting much. But the water began to stir, and the boat began to jerk and dip. Simon started to pull up his net, and to his amazement, it was so full of fish he couldn't even lift it.

James and John, his business partners in another boat, had to row out and help. The nets tore as they lifted them, but even though some of their haul escaped, they filled both boats to the brim with fish—so much that the boats even started to sink.

Suddenly, Simon realized he was in the presence of a holy man. Jesus's teaching was great, but this was something far more compelling. Something impossible was happening. Simon became deeply aware of his own brokenness and how he didn't deserve a blessing like this.

Simon flopped over the pile of fish and bowed at Jesus's knees. He begged Jesus to leave him alone, knowing he didn't deserve to be in the presence of someone like him.

Jesus answered him, "Don't be afraid—from now on you will fish for people."

What must Simon have thought? What must he have expected? I know what would have crossed my mind: *If this is what fishing for fish looks like to this guy, I can't imagine what fishing for people will be like!*

Simon, James, and John immediately left everything and began to follow Jesus.[1]

---

[1] The details of this story are adapted from Luke 5:1–11.

Learning from Jesus

Jesus called his followers disciples. A disciple is a learner. In the case of Christianity, disciples are daily committed to learning from Jesus—being transformed into his likeness in their thoughts, attitudes, desires, emotions, words, behavior, and overall lifestyle.

As theologian Dallas Willard puts it, "Discipleship is the process of becoming who Jesus would be if he were you"[2] If Jesus grew up in your circumstances—with your education, your genetics, your friends, your family (or lack thereof)—and lived in your current situation, how would he live?

To put it another way, the "death" and new life we talked about in the last chapter don't mean you lose your uniqueness and become some sort of Jesus-drone. Instead, you become a unique expression of Jesus. You shine his love and goodness with your own distinctive creativity, skills, sense of humor, strengths, weaknesses, preferences, and more.

Even with all those unique variables, we know a few things about Jesus that would remain consistent, regardless of circumstances. He would live self-sacrificially. He would love and care for the disenfranchised. He would heal the sick, raise the dead, and drive evil spiritual forces away from anyone who was oppressed. He would teach people how to know his Father. He would serve humbly, love faithfully, give generously, and so on.

And that's who he wants to be in you.

The way Jesus does it is through "union." Jesus puts his Holy Spirit in you, giving you access to his thoughts, desires, hopes, and demeanor. He links up with you and teaches you to live like he does.

Jesus once said, "Come to me, all you who are weary and burdened, and I will give you rest. Take my yoke upon

---

[2] Dallas Willard, "Why Bother with Discipleship?" *Dallas Willard*, accessed on February 13, 2022, www.dwillard.org/articles/artview.asp?artID=71.

ROOTED

you and learn from me, for I am gentle and humble in heart, and you will find rest for your souls. For my yoke is easy and my burden is light."[3]

In today's world, most of us are unfamiliar with yokes. Perhaps you've seen an old picture of two oxen with a shaped wooden plank across their shoulders, somehow looped around their necks. Typically, a chain or pole stretches back between the oxen, perhaps attached to a cart, a plow, or some other piece of farming equipment. By pulling together as a team, the two oxen can accomplish exponentially more than a single ox, though there are also yokes made for individual animals to do light labor.

In the Bible times, sometimes even people would wear yokes over their shoulders to help them gain the leverage needed to pull a heavy load.[4] The concept of a yoke implied work, service, and subjection to another. Most of the time, when yokes are mentioned metaphorically in the Bible, the implications are negative. But in this case, Jesus calls his yoke "easy" and says that his followers will find rest for their souls.

When Jesus invited his listeners to take his yoke upon them, he was most likely talking about his teaching. Unlike the rules and regulations that had oppressed the people under the teachings of various religious leaders at the time, Jesus offered a new way of life. Instead of policing people's behavior with external rules, he would transform people into new creations who would naturally do the right thing.

Jesus's teaching isn't burdensome; it's transformative.

No matter how many times you tell a cat to bark like a dog, it can't. That's simply not how cats are designed. But suppose there were some way to magically transform a cat into a dog. Suddenly, barking would be normal and natural.

---

[3] Matthew 11:28–30.
[4] Joachim Jeremias, *The Parables of Jesus*, second revised edition, (Norwich, UK: SCM Press, 1972), 194.

22

When Paul wrote about Christian virtues like love, joy, peace, patience, and self-control, he called them fruit.[5] Trees don't have to strive or work hard to produce fruit. Trees simply need good soil, water, and sunlight. The fruit is produced naturally and effortlessly.

Likewise, we who follow Jesus have an advantage called grace. Grace is God's undeserved favor toward us that enables us to do things together with him that would be impossible to do on our own. When we humble ourselves enough to declare, "I'm not strong enough to live for God by myself," he responds by giving us grace.[6] Suddenly, we find ourselves living for God with greater ease—still needing to make difficult decisions, still needing to serve people, and still needing to do hard things but now with special strength that comes from God.[7]

Newborn Disciples

Remember that yoke? It does no good to slap a yoke on a couple of cows and see what happens. Some people don't know this, but an ox is not a unique species of animal. There's no such thing as a baby ox. The title of "ox" is only bestowed on a steer that has been trained and worked for four years. And that training doesn't start late in life. Rather, it usually begins when the animal is only a few weeks old.[8]

While it is true that Jesus will receive us as we are, he doesn't leave us that way. He makes us new. The work to which he has called us requires us to do things differently than we ever have. Old habits need to die—habits of how we

---

[5] See Galatians 5:22–23.
[6] See James 4:6–10 and 2 Corinthians 12:9.
[7] See Colossians 1:29 and 1 Peter 4:11.
[8] "Training New Oxen," *Living History Farms*, January 5, 2015, www.lhf.org/2015/01/training-new-oxen.

ROOTED

respond to offense, how we treat our enemies, and how we prioritize our lives. Even the way we work needs to change. Everything in God's kingdom is backwards to what we've been taught. We die to live. We give to gain more. We bless those who attack us. Jesus said, "For whoever wants to save their life will lose it, but whoever loses their life for me and for the gospel will save it."[9]

Those who raise oxen start training calves as babies because the young ones haven't yet learned the bad habits of independence that would keep them from effectively working as a team. Similarly, Jesus said, "Very truly I tell you, no one can see the kingdom of God unless they are born again."[10]

You may not realize it, but when you considered your old life dead with Jesus and received his Holy Spirit, making you a new creation, you were "born again." That's what this term means.

Remember Simon the fisherman? Jesus later changed his name to Peter (which means "rock") because of the realization he had that Jesus was the Son of God.[11] Years later, Peter helped lead the first Christians. In a letter he wrote to Christians all around Asia Minor (now mostly found in Turkey), Peter said, "Like newborn babies, crave pure spiritual milk, so that by it you may grow up in your salvation, now that you have tasted that the Lord is good."[12]

You might not like the imagery of being like a baby, but it's the best way to think of yourself as you start out the Christian life. It's okay to see yourself as helpless because God will protect you. It's okay to see yourself as incapable because all our capability comes from God's grace. It's okay to recognize that you don't know much of anything because

---

9 Mark 8:35.
10 John 3:3.
11 See Matthew 16:13–20.
12 1 Peter 2:2–3.

that's the sort of curiosity needed to learn from Jesus and develop in your faith. Christian maturity doesn't come from putting on a face and pretending like you now have your life together. Christian maturity comes from staying humble and learning to trust God and his people like you never have before.

Taking Your First Step

When my first son took his first step on his own, he stood by the couch, wobbled a little, stretched one leg out in front of the other, leaned forward, planted his foot, and promptly fell to the ground. A baby's first step is somehow both natural and a thoughtful, effort-filled process. But now that my son was motivated to walk, my wife and I suddenly became intentional about calling him toward us, cheering him on at every attempt, and celebrating every new inch of distance he covered.

As Jesus's disciples, "walking" looks like "obedience." John wrote, "We know that we have come to know him if we keep his commands."[13] And just like Jesus said about his yoke, that it was "easy" and "light," John later added, "In fact, this is love for God: to keep his commands. And his commands are not burdensome, for everyone born of God overcomes the world."[14]

As a new creation, born of God, it's easy to obey God. His Spirit lives in you. You've been given his grace to enable you to live differently than you ever could in your own strength. Obedience is easy when Jesus lives in you.

If "walking" looks like "obedience," then what does it look like to take your first wobbly step? The Bible calls it "baptism." The very first act of obedience that Jesus expects from a new believer is to be baptized in water.

---

[13] 1 John 2:3.
[14] 1 John 5:3–4.

Perhaps your parents were part of a church that believed it is important to baptize infants. If so, they may have taken you to their church on a special day and had the priest, vicar, or pastor sprinkle some water on your head and pray a blessing. That's a wonderful act, and that blessing may have been a seed that has now grown into faith. But that's not the sort of baptism that has anything to do with obedience.

Peter called baptism "the pledge of a clear conscience toward God."[15] Babies don't make pledges. In fact, their consciences aren't even developed yet. Along those lines, Scripture calls water baptism a "baptism of repentance."[16] You may remember from the last chapter that to repent is to change the way you think. So if you were baptized as a baby, I wouldn't go so far as to say that it was a waste of time or meaningless, but I would encourage you to now be baptized as a personal choice—a first act of obedience in following Jesus.

Why would Jesus make this our first act of obedience? It's obviously easy to do, but that can't be the *only* reason.

The answer is found in the meaning and imagery of water baptism. The word *baptize* means "to immerse in or wash with water."[17] It implies complete submersion. As a person goes down into the water, they do so identifying with Jesus's death and burial—considering their old life dead. And then that person is lifted back up from the water just as Jesus was raised from the dead. Baptism is a powerful picture of the transformation that happened inside you when you believed in Jesus.

This first act of obedience is a resounding yes to Jesus. It's similar to a wedding. A wedding is an event that two people can look at as the moment their commitment was

---

[15] See 1 Peter 3:21.

[16] See Mark 1:4; Luke 3:3; Acts 13:24; and 19:4.

[17] Jerome H. Neyrey, Paul J. Achtemeier, general ed., "Baptism," *Harper's Bible Dictionary* (San Francisco: HarperSanFrancisco, 1985), 92–93.

officially ratified, so baptism is an event that we can look at as the moment our old life was unquestionably buried. Both weddings and baptisms require that we persevere in our commitment. Both mark life-altering moments that will change everything about how we live.

If you have never been baptized, ask the person who led you to Jesus if they can baptize you. If you don't know how to reach them or if they are unable to do so, find another mature Christian, such as a pastor.

Wear something you don't mind getting wet, such as a swimsuit.[18] Find some water. It doesn't matter if it's a lake, a swimming pool, a horse trough, or a bathtub. I have baptized people in the Indian Ocean, and I have baptized people in the tarp-lined bed of a pickup-truck. As long as it's deep enough to get your body underwater, it's great.

You and your friend will enter the water. There isn't really a script for what to say, but I'll usually ask, "Are you ready to follow Jesus for the rest of your life, no matter the cost?" Perhaps the person baptizing you will say something similar. After the person being baptized agrees, I'll usually say something like, "Then based on your profession of faith, I now baptize you in the name of the Father and the Son and the Holy Spirit."[19]

Plug your nose, and let the person help you tip back into the water. Then they'll lift you up, and it's time to celebrate.

---

[18] For the sake of modesty and minimizing distractions or "wardrobe malfunctions," some churches provide or encourage T-shirts or robes that more fully clothe people as they're baptized.

[19] Some Christians only baptize "in the name of Jesus," but in Matthew 28:19, Jesus instructed us to invoke all three persons of the holy Trinity when baptizing new believers in water.

ROOTED

What Next?

Once you've taken that first step, you're well on your way to walking. But just like a toddler, there's still a lot to learn. We need to be taught to obey Jesus.[20]

You will continue to learn from Jesus in three important ways. First is through his people. I'll share more in the next chapter about what church should be like and how you can get connected. Second is through personal dialogue with God called prayer. I'll teach you how to pray and recognize God's voice in chapter 4. And third is reading the Bible.

If you don't have a Bible yet, you can buy one at almost any store that sells books. They're also readily available online. In fact, you can read the Bible for free through apps like YouVersion or websites like BibleGateway.com.

There are many different English translations of the Bible. I usually recommend the New International Version (NIV). It is translated by a team of brilliant scholars and is easy to understand. If you have a difficulty with reading comprehension, you'll find shorter sentences and an easier reading level in the New Living Translation (NLT). Either of these would be great as you're getting started.

If you're not familiar with the Bible, have a look at the table of contents. There, you'll find sixty-six different books, divided into two parts—thirty-nine in the Old Testament and twenty-seven in the New Testament.

The Old Testament is essentially the Jewish Scriptures, which Jesus and his followers would have read. Many authors wrote these Scriptures as the Holy Spirit directed and inspired them. Some are history, some are poetry, and some are direct messages from God to his people, spoken through prophets. Many of the prophecies point to a coming Savior, and Jesus fulfilled every single one of those prophecies. The Old

---

[20] Matthew 28:20.

Testament is great to read, but it's probably not the best place to start. In fact, I would read the entire New Testament first.

The New Testament starts with four books named after their authors: Matthew, Mark, Luke, and John. These are called the four Gospels. Each is an account of Jesus's life. The first three are similar to each other and share a lot of the same stories, some with different details. The fourth one—John—is unique and focuses more on the fact that Jesus is God.

In most cases, I recommend people start by reading Mark. It's action-packed, full of emotion, and easy to read. It's also the shortest of the four Gospels. If you come from a Jewish background, you might want to start by reading Matthew. And if you're the sort of person who wants all the details, you may prefer reading Luke.

When you're done reading one of the Gospels, read the next book, called Acts. This is a historical account of the first Christians. It includes extreme miracles, intense persecution, and wonderful testimonies about what following Jesus looks like.

The rest of the New Testament is composed of letters that were written to various churches and individuals. You'll especially want to look at Romans, Ephesians, Colossians, James, and 1 John—mostly just because these are my favorites—but really, all the New Testament is great for various reasons.

Thumbing through the Bible, you'll find big numbers and small numbers. The big numbers are the chapters, and the little numbers are the verses. So for example, if you want to find Galatians 2:20, first turn to the book of Galatians, then find the big number "2" and scan down to the little number "20." Then you can read the verse referenced.

From time to time, you will inevitably come across passages that don't make sense to you. I'm a pastor, and this still happens to me. A good Bible commentary can sometimes help you understand what you're reading. Commentaries are written by scholars who have doctorate degrees in the original

languages and have devoted their lives to studying the Bible
and history and explaining it to people. Remember the
chapter and number of the verse you want to understand, and
you can then look it up in order in the commentary.

There are hundreds of commentaries, and some are
better than others. For someone getting started, I recommend
the *IVP Bible Background Commentary* by InterVarsity Press. The
New Testament volume is written by a brilliant scholar named
Craig Keener. I recommend buying that first if it sounds
interesting to you. The Old Testament volume is good too, but
I find myself not using that one nearly as often, so you
probably don't need it to start. You can order both on
Amazon.

I encourage people to highlight in their Bibles whenever
they find something that stands out to them. The pages of
most Bibles are thin, though, so be careful about ink bleeding
through the pages. Some people prefer to underline with
colored pencils for this reason. Personally, I like the Sharpie
brand Liquid Highlighter. It does a great job of putting bold
color on the page without bleeding.

And when a verse impacts you deeply, I recommend
trying to memorize it. Handwrite it several times. Read it out
loud. Practice reciting it until you've locked it into your
memory.

It's best to discuss what you're reading with Christians
who have been studying the Bible longer than you. They may
have some of the same questions you do, but group-
interpretation tends to be more accurate than individual
interpretation. Some people know other parts of the Bible
better than you do, and they can help with the nuances of
what you're reading.

Find a small group of Christians who are interested in
studying the Bible together. Approach the text humbly, not
assuming that you'll have all the answers. I often joke that I
disagree with five-years-ago-me, which means I'll probably
disagree with five-years-from-now-me. And I'm still not sure

which one is right about everything, but it's probably not right-now-me. Some Scripture is plain in its meaning, but some deserves a lifetime of study. Commit yourself to studying the Bible with a small group of Christians who want to learn new things from Jesus, and you'll be in good company.

ROOTED

CHAPTER 3

WELCOME TO THE FAMILY

Yet to all who did receive him, to those who believed in his name, he gave the right to become children of God—children born not of natural descent, nor of human decision or a husband's will, but born of God.

—JOHN 1:12–13

My wife went into labor, but our baby wasn't due for another five-and-a-half weeks. We raced to the hospital, where they tried to stop her labor, but soon Josiah was on his way.

To spare you some details that aren't relevant to my point, Josiah was born that day via an emergency C-section. While my wife, Robin, was still recovering from anesthesia, I sat awake all night in the Neonatal Intensive Care Unit (NICU), watching my little baby struggle uncomfortably in an incubator. He slept almost the entire time, but I sat there for hours, just watching and praying for him. Sometimes I would gently hum a worship song. My heart was overwhelmed with joy and gratitude.

I didn't sleep. I didn't eat. I couldn't pry myself away from my little baby boy.

Sometime in the middle of the night, a realization washed over me. In awe, I looked at my little baby and prayed, "Wow. I think I finally get it. This is how you love me, God!"

There was nothing my son could do for me. He couldn't clean my house, wash my car, or pay me rent. All he knew how to do was sleep, cry, and make little messes that I had to clean up.

And yet, I was wildly in love with him.

God's love for us is not based on our performance. It's based on the fact that we're his children.

> For I am convinced that neither death nor life, neither angels nor demons, neither the present nor the future, nor any powers, neither height nor depth, nor anything else in all creation, will be able to separate us from the love of God that is in Christ Jesus our Lord.[1]

There's a reason Jesus revealed God as Father. God's kingdom is a family. Our Father loves us, cares for us, and provides for us. We're not orphans. We're not on our own. We have a destiny and a future. We don't need to worry about anything.

Some people have grown up without fathers or with men who set poor examples of fatherhood for them. For such people, the thought of God as Father can be scary or foreign. But those broken people do not define fatherhood. God does. We wouldn't even be able to talk about those who failed as fathers if there weren't the one perfect Father against whom we could compare them.

Even if you've never known an earthly father or even if father figures in your life were abusive or neglectful, you can know God as the good Father that he is. If you ask him to reveal his love to you, he will. He's watching over you right now, just like I watched over my newborn son. His affection toward you is beyond your comprehension.

Before you read any further, I want you to close your eyes and pray out loud, "Father, I am precious to you." Then

---

[1] Romans 8:38–39.

take a minute to be present in the moment. Let yourself feel the weight of that truth. Let yourself feel his love for you.

The Divine Family

Jesus is fascinating. He is somehow both human and divine. He is God in the flesh.[2] And yet he is also "fully human in every way."[3]

How is Jesus somehow both God and also "the Son of God"? Theologians have called this principle a mystery for centuries. I'm not going to solve it for you in a few paragraphs, but I'll offer you a few ideas that help me think about it.

Suppose I have a voicemail on my phone. I start listening to it. My friend asks who called me, and I answer, "It's my wife."

Is it actually my wife? In a sense, yes. In another sense, it's just her voice. But my wife's voice is an expression of my wife's heart. It reveals her thoughts and personality. Hearing my wife's voice is exactly the same as hearing my wife. And if I call her back, I'll interact with her by interacting with her voice. Nevertheless, I'm married to all of my wife, not only her voice. Her voice is 100 percent her. But she is also more than just a voice.

Jesus is called the Word of God.[4] The Bible says that Jesus existed before anything was ever created,[5] and it describes him as being the one who actually did the creating.[6] But when you read the biblical account of creation, how is God described creating things? He spoke everything into existence.[7]

---

[2] See John 1:1 and 1:14.
[3] Hebrews 2:17.
[4] John 1:1.
[5] See Colossians 1:17.
[6] See John 1:3 and Colossians 1:16.
[7] See Genesis 1.

Jesus—the Word of God—has eternally proceeded from the Father. He has always been one with Father God, and yet he has also always been somehow distinct, just as my wife's voice is her and yet also distinct from her at the same time.

It's not a perfect analogy, but it's how God has chosen to reveal himself to us.

> In the past God spoke to our ancestors through the prophets at many times and in various ways, but in these last days he has spoken to us by his Son, whom he appointed heir of all things, and through whom also he made the universe. The Son is the radiance of God's glory and the exact representation of his being, sustaining all things by his powerful word. After he had provided purification for sins, he sat down at the right hand of the Majesty in heaven.[8]

Somehow, Jesus is fully God and yet is also seated at the right hand of the Father in heaven. And then there's another divine person called the Holy Spirit. Sometimes he is called the Spirit of the Father.[9] Sometimes he is called the Spirit of Christ.[10] And sometimes he is just called God.[11] I'll tell you more about the Holy Spirit in a couple of chapters, but for now, simply know that he is God too, just like the Father and the Son. Somehow all three—Father, Son, and Holy Spirit— are each entirely God and yet also distinct from each other.

When Jesus was baptized in water, Father God spoke audibly from heaven, and the Holy Spirit descended on Jesus like a dove.[12] Jesus regularly spoke about the Father and the Holy Spirit as being different persons than himself, and yet he

---

[8] Hebrews 1:1–3
[9] See Matthew 10:19–20 (contrast with Mark 13:11).
[10] See Acts 16:7; Galatians 4:6; and Philippians 1:19.
[11] See Acts 5:3–4.
[12] See Luke 3:21–22.

also said, "I and the Father are one," and, "Anyone who has seen me has seen the Father."[13]

Again, it's a mystery, but it's beautiful to think about because it has incredible meaning for us. God is one being but is also somehow a plurality of three persons, each of whom is the fullness of God. This means that although God is only one being in his essence, he has always existed in a sort of divine family. This reveals to us that God's nature is relational harmony. John went so far as to write that "God is love."[14]

That means God didn't "need" to create us. He wasn't lonely, all by himself, before creation. God was complete—the embodiment of relational harmony, peace, and love. God created us not to fill some inner void but simply because he wanted to. His love is so abundant that it's only logical he would create new people on whom he could pour out his affection. You exist because our all-loving God decided he liked the idea of eternity with you better than eternity without you—not so much for his own fulfillment but for yours.

God is perfect, but we are not. And his perfection is so intense that any imperfect thing would be obliterated in his presence. But Father God sent his Son, Jesus, in the power of the Holy Spirit, to wash away all our sin and make us righteous—people who could live in harmony with him. God has done all the work and welcomed you into his divine family. He has sent the Holy Spirit—the Spirit of his Son—into your heart, enabling you to call God "Father."[15]

---

[13] John 10:30 and John 14:9, respectively.

[14] See 1 John 4:16.

[15] See Galatians 4:4–7. We're not only invited to call God "Father" but "Abba," which is an Aramaic term of endearment that a young child would use when addressing their dad. Kenneth E. Bailey, *Jesus through Middle Eastern Eyes: Cultural Studies in the Gospels* (Westmont, Illinois: InterVarsity Press, 2008), 94.

Yet to all who did receive him, to those who believed in his name, he gave the right to become children of God—children born not of natural descent, nor of human decision or a husband's will, but born of God.[16]

As someone who has put your faith in Jesus, you have been welcomed into God's family. You have been invited into his abundant love and relational harmony. You can think of your "family tree" as a "family stick"—no branches, just God and you, alongside billions of brothers and sisters from throughout the ages. The Bible declares, "See what great love the Father has lavished on us, that we should be called children of God. And that is what we are!"[17]

The Apple Doesn't Fall Far from the Tree

Jesus once called a group of people "children of the devil" because they were doing what the devil did—lying and trying to kill him.[18] He said, "If you were Abraham's children, then you would do what Abraham did."[19] According to Jesus, you can tell who someone is allowing to "father" them by who they most resemble.

The words above were recorded by John—one of Jesus's followers and one of the original fishermen who Jesus invited to fish for people. Later, John said the following in one of the letters he wrote:

Dear children, do not let anyone lead you astray. The one who does what is right is righteous, just as he is righteous. The one who does what is sinful is of the

---

[16] John 1:12–13.
[17] 1 John 3:1.
[18] See John 8:44–47.
[19] See John 8:39.

devil, because the devil has been sinning from the beginning. The reason the Son of God appeared was to destroy the devil's work. No one who is born of God will continue to sin, because God's seed remains in them; they cannot go on sinning, because they have been born of God. This is how we know who the children of God are and who the children of the devil are: Anyone who does not do what is right is not God's child, nor is anyone who does not love their brother and sister.[20]

That Scripture may seem like an impossibly high standard, but it's a great reminder that we were made for more than "life as usual."[21] Thankfully, Jesus meets that impossibly high standard for us, expressing his own love and obedience through us via the Holy Spirit who lives in us.

I'm still learning how to reveal Jesus more fully than I already do. I want people to experience him when they experience me. Sometimes I'm better at surrendering to him than other times. But I'm more like Jesus today than I was twenty years ago, and I expect that trajectory to continue. It's natural to do what my Father does.

One thing I have learned about my Father in heaven is that his outrageous love is poured out toward people in various ways. To those who don't know him, he sent his Son, Jesus, to save them from their sins and bring them into his family. If

---

[20] 1 John 3:7–10.

[21] It should be noted that John said he wrote this letter "so that you will not sin," which means he believed this teaching would help people live righteously. (See 1 John 2:1.) But he also presented a backup plan: "But if anybody does sin, we have an advocate with the Father—Jesus Christ the Righteous One" (1 John 2:1). In other words, don't get down on yourself if you make a mistake. Simply receive God's forgiveness and move forward. We ought to live our lives expecting to look more and more like Jesus in our words, actions, and attitudes.

I'm like my Father, then I, too, want to sacrifice for those who don't know him and share the good news about what Jesus has done, inviting people into our family. For us who do know him, he loves to speak with us, spend time with us, and help us when we need him. If I'm like my Father, then I want to be around other Christians, speaking to them, loving them, and serving them.

This is what we call "church."

You Are Not Alone

When Jesus gathered his first followers, he started with a small group of men and women. Jesus never intended for us to follow him alone. He has always gathered believers in groups, sending out no fewer than two at a time, and always bringing them back to a larger team.

The word "church" is often thought of as a special building, and that may actually be the origin of the English word.[22] But in the Bible, the original Greek word that we translate as "church" was less specific and referred to a gathering of people who could be identified together.

In other words, there's no such thing as being a Christian and subscribing to a lone-wolf lifestyle of "just Jesus and me." God intends for us—as members of his one big, timeless, global, heavenly family—to gather with other Christians in small, nuclear families.[23] He wants us to love, encourage, challenge, strengthen, correct, serve, teach, and learn from each other.

If you're a child of God, then you want to be with other Christians. That's what your Father wants to do, and you're

---

[22] Shayne Looper, "Looper Column: The Curious Origin of the Word 'Church,'" *The Register-Guard*, Northwest Florida Daily News, March 13, 2020, https://www.registerguard.com/opinion/20200313/looper-column-curious-origin-of-word-church.

[23] See Psalm 68:6 and Hebrews 10:24–25.

becoming like him. If you don't yet have a healthy church to attend, I highly recommend reaching out to the person who gave you this book. (Hopefully, that person wrote down their name and contact information on the last page.)

Some people attend church gatherings in large buildings designed specifically for that purpose. Some churches gather in schools. My own church gathers in people's homes (we call them "house churches"). It really doesn't matter what the venue is; the church is people who have united in mission and purpose as they follow Jesus.

You belong in a church. You don't have to wait until you're more perfect. Churches are full of imperfect people. That means sometimes people will say or do things they shouldn't as they're still learning to follow Jesus. But that doesn't mean you should be guarded. If people hurt you, the Holy Spirit lives in you to comfort you and heal your heart. Open up your heart to truly love people and let them love you.

You want to be in a church that has some sort of small group ministry available—some place where Christians can be interactive, discuss the Bible, be vulnerable, care and pray for each other, and so on. Large gatherings are great and exciting, but much of what the Bible tells us to do in church is only possible in a small group of about five to twenty people.[24]

When you gather meaningfully with other believers, you'll learn to worship God, study the Bible, and serve God's mission of reaching new people with the message of Jesus. You'll also find that you're not alone as you're trying to follow Jesus. You'll build deep and lasting friendships. You'll find people who will mentor you in your faith. And you'll soon find others whom you can mentor. This is how we all grow together to look more like Jesus.[25]

---

[24] See Acts 2:42–47; 1 Corinthians 14:26–31; and Hebrews 10:25.
[25] See Ephesians 4:11–15.

Revealing Jesus Together

Church gatherings are more than family reunions; they're opportunities to learn from Jesus together. The Bible says that the Holy Spirit specially empowers each person to reveal something different from Jesus.[26] So when we gather and lovingly share these expressions of Jesus for the sake of others, we see a fuller picture emerge of who Jesus is and what he wants to communicate to us as a group. The Holy Spirit might give special grace to one person to share a message of wisdom. He might empower someone else to bring a miracle of physical healing to someone who needs it. He might enable another to teach something from the Scriptures and another to recognize what God wants to say to everyone in the room (we call this "prophecy").

When small church gatherings operate like this, the entire gathering becomes an experience with Jesus. People walk away refreshed and equipped to share Jesus with friends, family, coworkers, classmates, neighbors, and strangers.

As I write this, my baby son in the NICU is now eleven years old and thriving. I'm still just as crazy in love with him. He sometimes stands like I do, talks like I do, jokes like I do, acts like I do, and more. Some of that may be genetics. Some of that may be time spent together. There is no question that he is my son.

The one who embodies love is our Father, and we're learning to be like him. Our lives are being molded into his image and likeness. We are becoming the embodiment of love on earth, such that when people encounter us, they encounter him. And we do all this together as a family. This is what it means to be children of God.

---

[26] See 1 Corinthians 12:4–27.

CHAPTER 4

TALKING WITH GOD

My sheep listen to my voice;
I know them, and they follow me.
I give them eternal life, and they shall never perish;
no one will snatch them out of my hand.

—JOHN 10:27–28

The whole reason you were created was so that you could enjoy God in a loving relationship. Even though he enjoys you, he didn't create you out of a need for enjoyment. As mentioned in the previous chapter, God was complete throughout all eternity past. But as a God of love, he generously gives of himself, longing for you to experience all his goodness. You were designed to know him.

My parents showed me what a relationship with God looks like. From the time I was a baby, when my mom would sing worship songs instead of lullabies, I grew up in a family that daily interacted with God.

I often found my mom kneeling in her room with her eyes clenched, praying out loud. Sometimes, she wrote her prayers in a journal. She often led Bible studies for women in our church, guiding them into powerful times of prayer together.

My dad was a car salesman. I know that doesn't sound like a very spiritual career, but Dad saw it as a ministry. As a child, I often came into my parents' room early in the morning and found my dad sitting on the edge of his bed, praying for his family, church, friends, and business. While at work, even though he earned money on commission, he often took extra time with customers, sharing stories about the many miracles God had done in his life. Many times, he prayed with people at his desk.

After work, we all ate dinner together, and Dad told us how the Holy Spirit spoke to him at work. Each story either included the miraculous results because he heeded that voice or, sometimes, the disastrous results because he didn't listen.

My dad became one of the top Ford salesmen in the United States. He was selling so many cars that my mom started working alongside him. She prepped cars, traded cars with other dealerships, played with children while their parents signed papers, and more. And Dad would do the selling. Many times, Mom counseled or pray with ladies in the office—sometimes even with customers. My parents were respectful and kind to the mechanics and those in the service department. They became a sort of Mom and Dad to everyone at the dealership.

My parents demonstrated that you don't have to be a pastor or paid minister to have a meaningful relationship with God. They were successful businesspeople, not because they took advantage of people but because they knew that loving God and loving people were the two most important activities in life.[1]

When my parents were at work, I didn't go to day care; I went to Grandma's house. My dad's mom was also a woman of prayer. I rarely ever saw Grandma having a long, intentional prayer time like I saw my dad do in the mornings, but she talked out loud to Jesus like he was a friend standing right next to her. She asked him questions, and then thoughts

---

[1] See Mark 12:28–31.

came to her that hadn't occurred to her before. And just like my dad, she too talked about the still, small voice of God that reminded her to turn the oven off or showed her how to fix something or warned her about rain coming or helped her understand the Bible.

My family taught me some incredible things about a lifestyle of prayer:

* ❖ Prayer doesn't require a script or liturgy.
* ❖ Prayer doesn't require fancy words.
* ❖ Prayer is a two-way conversation, not a one-way monologue.
* ❖ God will speak with us about anything—not only the big, important stuff.
* ❖ God's voice is as near to you as your own thoughts, and recognizing him takes sensitivity and intentionality.
* ❖ You're never too busy to pray. If anything, you're too busy not to pray.
* ❖ Prayer works because God works, and he loves you.

How Jesus Taught Us to Pray

Jesus taught his disciples something we often call "the Lord's prayer." If you grew up in a traditional church (Catholic or Lutheran, for example), you may have heard this prayer recited regularly:

> Our Father in heaven,
>   hallowed be your name,
> your kingdom come,
> your will be done,
>   on earth as it is in heaven.
> Give us today our daily bread.
> And forgive us our debts,
>   as we also have forgiven our debtors.

And lead us not into temptation,
    but deliver us from the evil one.[2]

It's great to recite this prayer, but it's even more important to understand what it means. It's not a list of magic words with power in and of themselves. It's an invitation to trust God for everything in life.

The prayer starts with "Our Father in heaven." Although this prayer is recorded for us in Greek, most scholars today agree that Jesus would have spoken this prayer in the common person's language of Aramaic, making the first word "Abba."[3]

In some cultures, still today, "abba" is the first word many children say. A similar two-syllable word in English might be "dada," as many toddlers call their fathers. But unlike dada, the word "abba" could be used throughout life. In English, this is a little more like how some daughters might call their fathers "Daddy" well into their teen or adult years. It's a term of endearment and implies a close, meaningful relationship.

God wants you to know him as a perfect dad. So Jesus taught us to approach God in prayer with this truth at the forefront of our minds.

But lest we become unhealthily chummy with our heavenly Dad, the next line reminds us that he is still God. "Hallowed be your name." We don't often use this word in English, but "hallowed" means to be greatly revered and honored. It implies something is sacred or special—unlike anything else. God is so perfect and awe-striking that even his name is holy.

In other words, Jesus taught us to approach God both affectionately and worshipfully. Sometimes I'll take a moment

---

[2] Matthew 6:9–13.
[3] Bailey, *Jesus through Middle Eastern Eyes*, 94.

to make myself aware of how amazing and powerful he is. Sometimes I'll sing to him. Most of the time, I simply take time to express gratitude to him. I usually start my prayers with, "Father, thank you for ..." As one of the Bible's poets wrote:

> Enter his gates with thanksgiving
>   and his courts with praise;
>   give thanks to him and praise his name.
> For the Lord is good and his love endures forever;
>   his faithfulness continues through all generations.[4]

The next part of the prayer Jesus taught says, "Your kingdom come, your will be done, on earth as it is in heaven."

To put it another way, everything that happens in God's domain—his heavenly kingdom—is perfectly according to his will. Heaven does not have any sick people, hungry people, bitter people, hurting people, and so on. Everyone there has been made healthy and whole, physically, emotionally, and spiritually. In God's kingdom, there is no relational strife, economic distress, or lack of any kind. And Jesus taught us to pray that all the beauty of that perfect, heavenly world would invade the pain and chaos of this broken, earthly world.

Praying like this prepares us for miracles. As we invite his world to infiltrate our world, we see broken things made right. Lives are transformed. Just as God has been setting things right in your heart since you decided to follow Jesus, he begins to set things right in the world around you. That doesn't mean everything in your life will be perfect—we will still face many challenges. But it does mean that he will intervene in these situations—healing sick people, mending relationships, providing for physical needs, and more.

Everything else in the prayer Jesus modeled is an extension of this idea. We ask for "daily bread," which refers

---

[4] Psalm 100:4–5.

to the things we need right now, today, to live meaningfully for God. Sometimes this is literal food. Sometimes it's something less tangible, like wisdom. Whatever you need as you follow Jesus, God will provide. And this even includes such spiritual needs as forgiveness and the power to overcome temptation and spiritual oppression.

Much more could be said about this model prayer. Entire books have been written about it. But in summary, Jesus taught us to pray in a way that is personal, affectionate, reverent, and trusting. All these attributes together are called faith.

Faith Is a Relational Word

Perhaps you've heard the word "faith" used as a synonym for "religion" or "belief." Someone might say, "That person comes from a different faith." But actually, faith has a different meaning.

We understand this when we talk about human relationships. If I say I have faith in my wife, no one thinks I practice a religion that worships my wife. They simply understand that I trust her implicitly.

In fact, my trust in my wife is not merely a belief in my mind. I express it with my actions. I entrust her with money, possessions, and our children. I don't micromanage or control everything she does. I give her opportunities to demonstrate her faithfulness.

Having faith in God is not simply believing a list of statements about him. Having faith in God looks like entrusting your life to him. It looks like surrendering the natural tendency to try to control your own life and destiny.

In prayer, faith looks like more than believing God is real. Faith has more to do with trusting his nature—that he is good and wants to answer his children. The Bible puts it this way:

And without faith it is impossible to please God, because anyone who comes to him must believe that he exists and that he rewards those who earnestly seek him.[5]

Our trust in God's nature is directly related to the effectiveness of our prayers. James, another author in the Bible, writes:

> If any of you lacks wisdom, you should ask God, who gives generously to all without finding fault, and it will be given to you. But when you ask, you must believe and not doubt, because the one who doubts is like a wave of the sea, blown and tossed by the wind. That person should not expect to receive anything from the Lord. Such a person is double-minded and unstable in all they do.[6]

Remember that we're praying to Abba. He's wildly, madly in love with his kids. We pray to the God who really does want the best for us and is often waiting for us to simply ask.

As a father, sometimes my boys will ask for a snack right before dinner. I'll tell them no, not because I don't love my kids or want them to be happy. I tell them no because I know better food is coming, and a snack would rob them of enjoying it.

God doesn't want to answer some prayers, not because we're praying for the wrong things but because better things are coming. Other times, God doesn't want to answer prayers because as a good Father, he knows that to answer such a prayer would be bad for us.

---

[5] Hebrews 11:6.
[6] James 1:5–8.

For example, James also wrote:

> You do not have because you do not ask God. When you ask, you do not receive, because you ask with wrong motives, that you may spend what you get on your pleasures.[7]

As you can see, God wants us to ask him for things. But he wants us to ask with the right motives. He wants us to learn to love. And he doesn't want anything to get in the way of our eternity with him.

Knowing this and knowing his nature, we can learn to trust him no matter what is happening in our lives.

He is always good.

Always.

We can put our trust in no better person. God is always faithful. Paul wrote to his friend Timothy, "If we are faithless, he remains faithful."[8] So even when you're struggling to have the faith you need to pray meaningfully and effectively, God won't abandon you. Just because God prefers faith-filled prayers doesn't mean God turns his back on us when our faith is weak. He might not answer, but he withholds the answer as a loving Father, teaching us to trust.

You have nothing to worry about. Simply trust God. When you need more faith, ask him for it. When you need wisdom, ask him for it. When you need provision, ask him for it. When you need boldness, ask him for it. And if you're ever unsure why circumstances aren't going the way you expect, ask him about that too.

---

[7] James 4:2–3.
[8] 2 Timothy 2:13.

God Speaks

Yes, God will speak to you. You don't have to be a pastor or a prophet to hear God's voice. You could be a car salesperson like my dad. You could be at home most of the day like my grandmother. You could be a student like I was when I was learning to hear God's voice. It really doesn't matter. All Christians can hear God's voice.[9]

And God is frequently communicating with us in one way or another. The issue is not that we can't hear him; it's that we don't always recognize his voice.

Most people expect God's voice to boom in their ears. They expect to literally hear him speak. And while God did speak in an audible way like that a few times in the Bible, more often, God speaks more subtly.

As stated at the beginning of this chapter, the whole reason you were created was so that you could enjoy God in a loving relationship. Think about what that means. You were physiologically designed to have a relationship with him. It's the reason for your existence. That means hearing God's voice is one of the most natural things you'll ever experience. You were made for it.

Many Christians think they've never heard God's voice because they're waiting for the sky to rip open and a loud voice to boom out of the heavens. They believe that God's voice to them will be unnaturally obvious. But if God designed you to communicate with him, the opposite is more likely true.

In fact, every Christian has already heard and responded to God's voice at least once. Jesus said, "No one can come to me unless the Father who sent me draws them, and I will raise them up at the last day. It is written in the Prophets: 'They will all be taught by God.' Everyone who has heard the Father and

---

[9] John 10:27–28.

learned from him comes to me."[10] In other words, you wouldn't be a Christian if you hadn't heard God's voice.

But when you became a Christian, did God speak to you audibly? Probably not. While I have heard a few people in my life share such a testimony, it's certainly not typical. Most of us simply felt something deep inside, drawing us to Jesus. Perhaps it was a thought, affirming our need for a Savior. Perhaps it was a realization of our own unworthiness and sin. Perhaps it was a sudden desire to follow Jesus no matter the cost. Something inside us simply knew that the good news about Jesus was true. And that was God, speaking to us.

Subtle and Profound

God certainly speaks in some "loud" ways. Many have told stories of visions so vivid that they obscured their physical field of view. Others have told of an audible voice that shook them to their core. But in my personal experience, these sorts of encounters with God seem to be reserved for situations where God knows he needs to make himself extremely clear.

For example, centuries before Jesus came, when a man named Moses was solely responsible to lead God's people through the wilderness, God had to be incredibly obvious so that the people wouldn't be led astray. In the Old Testament book of Numbers, we read, "When there is a prophet among you, I, the Lord, reveal myself to them in visions, I speak to them in dreams. But this is not true of my servant Moses; he is faithful in all my house. With him I speak face to face, clearly and not in riddles; he sees the form of the Lord."[11]

In other words, the most common way God speaks is more subtle—visions, dreams, riddles, and so on. His voice might just seem like a passing thought or an image in your

---

[10] John 6:44–45.
[11] Numbers 12:6–8.

mind. It might even be a subtle physical sensation or a gut feeling.

Even when God speaks audibly, it's possible to miss what he's saying. Once, while Jesus was predicting his death, God spoke audibly, and some people still missed it.

> "Now my soul is troubled, and what shall I say? 'Father, save me from this hour'? No, it was for this very reason I came to this hour. Father, glorify your name!"
> Then a voice came from heaven, "I have glorified it, and will glorify it again." The crowd that was there and heard it said it had thundered; others said an angel had spoken to him.[12]

Why would God typically speak in a way that we could easily dismiss? Part of the answer, I suppose, is that he is less interested in controlling our lives and more interested in allowing us the privilege of choosing whether to listen for him.

God also loves hiding special things for you to find. Think about the joy of finding a love note in your lunchbox or a child searching for Easter eggs. God speaks loudly enough that we can hear, but he prefers not to speak so loudly that it robs us of the blessing found in faith.

Hearing Together

Not every thought that comes to you is God. Not every picture that races through your head is a message. Not every dream is his voice. That's why it's important to gather with other Christians to study the Bible and discuss what you all think you're hearing from him.

The Bible is the one and only ancient book that has stood the test of extreme scrutiny throughout the centuries and

---

[12] John 12:27–29

still proves reasonable and true. Some have tried to point out so-called flaws or inconsistencies in the Scriptures, but every one of these has a simple answer. Entire books have been written to prove the reliability of the Bible, and we can't address those matters here. So I will suggest that those with questions to do some deeper research. But if you're comfortable simply believing that the Bible is true, then we can move forward.

Peter wrote the following about the Scriptures:

> We also have the prophetic message as something completely reliable, and you will do well to pay attention to it, as to a light shining in a dark place, until the day dawns and the morning star rises in your hearts. Above all, you must understand that no prophecy of Scripture came about by the prophet's own interpretation of things. For prophecy never had its origin in the human will, but prophets, though human, spoke from God as they were carried along by the Holy Spirit.[13]

When we study the Bible, we learn what God's voice feels like. And when we study the Bible together with a group of Christians who agree on its authority, we are most likely to interpret it well and truly understand his voice.

With the Bible as a sort of anchor keeping us tethered to God's truth and with fellow Christians who have known God longer than we have, we can learn to hear his voice in the subjective matters of everyday life.

Talk with mature Christians about what you believe God might be saying. Be open to being corrected or challenged. Approach disagreements with love and humility. Even those of

---

[13] 2 Peter 1:19–21.

us who have been following Jesus for decades sometimes mistake our own thoughts for his.

Learning to hear God's voice is a lifelong pursuit. As you pray throughout your day, listen for God's response. Trust in his goodness. Pray with passion. Study the Scriptures. Dialogue with other Christians. Know God deeply.

ROOTED

CHAPTER 5:

REAL POWER

But you will receive power when the Holy Spirit comes on you; and you
will be my witnesses ... to the ends of the earth.

—ACTS 1:8

Do you remember what Jesus said he would teach Peter, James, and John to do? "'Come, follow me,' Jesus said, 'and I will send you out to fish for people.'"[1]

Following Jesus involves joining him in his mission. God wants to save the entire world.[2] Scripture shows us that he wants to accomplish this task in partnership with us, not alone.

But that sort of task is far too great for us. How could we ever possibly reach that many people? How could we have answers for all their questions? How could we bring hope to all the hopeless, healing to all the broken, and light to all those who are lost in their sin?

God has a solution: his Holy Spirit.

In chapter 3, I explained how our one God consists of the Father, the Son, and the Holy Spirit. Christian scholars call this the "Trinity." Each member of the Trinity is somehow both fully God and yet also distinct from the other two. In this chapter, I'm going to teach you more about the

---

[1] Matthew 4:19.
[2] See 2 Peter 3:9 and 1 Timothy 2:4.

Holy Spirit and show how he empowers us for the tremendous task of partnering with Jesus to save the world.

Who Is the Holy Spirit?

As I mentioned, the Holy Spirit is God and is one part of the Trinity, alongside the Father and the Son. He is the heavenly being who is eternally everywhere at once and has been active in the earth from the earliest moment of creation.

Still today, the Holy Spirit continues to be God's active presence in the earth, tangibly expressing the power and love of the Trinity. He is the one ultimately responsible for accomplishing the Father's will in the earth, and he does this by exalting Jesus, convicting the hearts of sinners, revealing what God is speaking, and partnering with willing humans to do whatever God desires.

The Holy Spirit is exactly what his name suggests: He is holy. That means he is entirely different from any created being and cannot be compared to anyone. He is also a spirit. That means he is a supernatural being—an immaterial but very real person who perfectly expresses the heart and will of Father God.

And most importantly, he wants to know you, and he wants you to know him.

The Holy Spirit Wants to Live inside of You

The Bible says that our physical bodies were designed by God to be living, breathing temples in which the Holy Spirit could dwell.

Do you not know that your bodies are temples of the Holy Spirit, who is in you, whom you have received from God? You are not your own; you were bought at a price. Therefore honor God with your bodies.[3]

---

[3] 1 Corinthians 6:19-20

This, of course, is only true for those who have experientially received salvation—trusting in Jesus's sacrifice to remove their sin and make them into new creations.

> And you also were included in Christ when you heard the message of truth, the gospel of your salvation. When you believed, you were marked in him with a seal, the promised Holy Spirit, who is a deposit guaranteeing our inheritance until the redemption of those who are God's possession—to the praise of his glory.[4]

Until Jesus died and rose again, the Holy Spirit was only *with* the disciples, not dwelling *inside* them. Jesus said:

> And I will ask the Father, and he will give you another advocate to help you and be with you forever—the Spirit of truth. The world cannot accept him, because it neither sees him nor knows him. But you know him, for he lives with you and will be in you. I will not leave you as orphans; I will come to you.[5]

When the Holy Spirit comes to live inside of you, he begins a work of transformation, changing you to become more and more like Jesus every day. This is what it means to be saved—it's not only about what happens after you die. It's about living in a meaningful relationship with God right now.[6]

---

[4] Ephesians 1:13–14.
[5] John 14:16–18. Notice Jesus said he would ask the Father, and he would send another person—the Holy Spirit. This is one of the ways we know the Father, Son, and Holy Spirit are distinct from each other. And yet, Jesus said, "I will come to you." This reminds us they are also one.
[6] See John 17:3.

ROOTED

The Holy Spirit Also Wants to Work outside You

The same Holy Spirit who loves to live inside you and bring transformation to your inner life also wants to bring transformation to the world around you.

Yes, he does some of this by transforming you into a person who loves and serves others with the nature of Jesus. But he also does things that don't have anything to do with how good or holy you are—working miracles through you, healing people, speaking to people through you, and more. When Peter worked a miracle, he told people that his own power or godliness did not make the crippled man walk.[7] Instead, the name of Jesus and the faith that comes through him worked through Peter.[8] The Holy Spirit can empower absolutely anyone—even those who are new to Christianity.

Long before Jesus died and rose again (enabling people to receive the Holy Spirit within them), God chose special men and women to empower. Most typically, the language used in the Bible is that the Holy Spirit "came upon" such people to enable them to do things beyond their natural ability.

❖ The Spirit came upon Moses to lead the people of Israel, and then he came upon the seventy elders of Israel to help Moses.[9]

❖ The Spirit came upon Balaam, and he prophesied.[10]

❖ The Spirit came upon Othniel, and he went to war.[11]

❖ The Spirit came upon Gideon, and he rallied the people for battle.[12]

---

[7] See Acts 3:12.
[8] See Acts 3:16.
[9] See Numbers 11:17.
[10] See Numbers 24:2.
[11] See Judges 3:10.
[12] See Judges 6:34.

❖ The Spirit came upon Samson, and he tore a lion in half.[13]
❖ The Spirit came upon Samson again, and he overcame thirty enemy soldiers.[14]
❖ On two occasions, the Spirit came upon King Saul, and he prophesied.[15]
❖ The Spirit came upon Saul's men, and they prophesied.[16]
❖ The same Holy Spirit who was on Elijah came on Elisha, and he carried on the ministry of miracles and prophecy.[17]

Even Jesus himself—although he was God in the flesh and certainly knew the Holy Spirit his entire life—did not begin ministering to other people, working miracles, or preaching until after the Holy Spirit came upon him.[18] This was part of his example to us.

Biblically, there appears to be a difference between what the Holy Spirit does *within* us (save, transform, and teach us) and what he does *upon* us (empower us for some earthly task).

Spiritual empowerment was rare in the time of the Old Testament. Only special people chosen by God could do things in the power of the Holy Spirit. But one prophet named Joel foresaw a time when God would put his Spirit upon all God's people—men, women, young, and old.[19] This is where the baptism in the Holy Spirit comes into action.

---

[13] See Judges 14:6.
[14] See Judges 14:19.
[15] See 1 Samuel 10:10 and 1 Samuel 19:23.
[16] See 1 Samuel 19:20.
[17] See 2 Kings 2:15.
[18] See Mark 1:9–11 and Acts 10:38.
[19] See Joel 2:28.

ROOTED

The Baptism in the Holy Spirit

John the Baptist prophesied that Jesus "will baptize you
with the Holy Spirit and fire."[20] Somehow, the same way John
baptized people in water, Jesus would baptize them in the
Holy Spirit.

Jesus explained when this would happen. Just before
Father God took him into heaven to sit on the throne at his
right hand, Jesus instructed his disciples, "Do not leave
Jerusalem, but wait for the gift my Father promised, which you
have heard me speak about. For John baptized with water, but
in a few days you will be baptized with the Holy Spirit."[21]

The timing of this event is important. Weeks earlier,
immediately following his resurrection, Jesus had already given
his disciples the Holy Spirit to dwell within them.[22] But here,
at the end of his earthly ministry, Jesus told the disciples to
wait for the Holy Spirit to clothe them with spiritual power.[23]
And he said they would receive this power when the Holy
Spirit comes "on" them.[24]

When the Holy Spirit came upon people in the Old
Testament, he did so to empower them for some earthly
task—most commonly to prophesy. Now, in the New
Testament, the Holy Spirit would come upon *all* believers to
empower us for our mission to partner with God in sharing the
message of Jesus with the whole world.

And then it happened. On a special Jewish feast day
called Pentecost, the Holy Spirit came to rest upon all the
believers present. A crowd formed, and Peter stood up to
address them. He pointed to Joel's prophecy in the Old
Testament, showing them that the Holy Spirit had been

---

[20] Matthew 3:11.
[21] Acts 1:4–5.
[22] See John 20:22.
[23] See Luke 24:49.
[24] See Acts 1:8.

poured out upon all the servants of God, empowering them to prophesy and declare the wonders of God as they engage in their global mission.[25]

The Symbolism of Pentecost

When the day of Pentecost came, they were all together in one place. Suddenly a sound like the blowing of a violent wind came from heaven and filled the whole house where they were sitting. They saw what seemed to be tongues of fire that separated and came to rest on each of them. All of them were filled with the Holy Spirit and began to speak in other tongues as the Spirit enabled them.[26]

The day of Pentecost was full of symbolism: a sound from heaven, something that looked like fire, spontaneous speech in unknown languages (we call this "speaking in tongues"), and more.

Today, when Jewish people celebrate the feast of Pentecost, they commemorate the day when God gave Moses the Law on Mt. Sinai. Note what happened at that event:

On the morning of the third day there was thunder and lightning, with a thick cloud over the mountain, and a very loud trumpet blast. Everyone in the camp trembled. Then Moses led the people out of the camp to meet with God, and they stood at the foot of the mountain. Mount Sinai was covered with smoke, because the Lord descended on it in fire. The smoke billowed up from it like smoke from a furnace, and the whole mountain trembled violently. As the

---

[25] See Acts 2:1–40.
[26] Acts 2:1–4.

sound of the trumpet grew louder and louder, Moses
spoke and the voice of God answered him.[27]

At Mt. Sinai, God set his people apart from the rest of
the world and gave them the law that Jewish people have
embraced for millennia. There was a sound from heaven. Fire
came to rest on the mountain, and then God spoke from the
mountain.

But Pentecost was different. As the sound from heaven
filled the house, fire came to rest on the people, and God
spoke from the people. Here, God again set his people apart
from the rest of the world. But instead of giving them a law
that they were powerless to fulfill, he gave them power in the
form of his own overwhelming presence. Jesus baptized them
in the Holy Spirit.

Pentecost was an annual celebration of the first fruits of
the wheat harvest—the first gathering of wheat each year,
which was offered to God, trusting that he would bless them
with far more during the rest of the growing season.

Interestingly, when Peter addressed the crowd, we see a
great harvest of souls take place as three thousand people were
baptized and joined the church. But this was only the first
fruits. A bountiful harvest was coming—one that would span
roughly two millennia and result in billions of Christians all
over the world today.

Why Tongues?

Why did the disciples speak in unknown languages on
the day of Pentecost? The simple answer is that's what God
wanted to do. But why? The Bible doesn't expressly tell us. We
can, however, infer a few things from Scripture. Among them
are the following three points:

---

[27] Exodus 19:16–19.

1. God had entrusted these empowered people with a message of good news for all nations.
2. God had empowered them to do the impossible.
3. God wanted everyone to know that time is short and the need is urgent.

Good News for All Nations: This first point ought to be obvious. Jesus had commanded his disciples to "go into all the world" and "make disciples of all nations."[28] But he had also told them not to go anywhere or do anything until they received the Spirit's empowerment.[29] Now that this power had been received, God gave them all an obvious sign that they were ready and empowered to go into all the world with his message of hope and salvation.

Power for the Impossible: Early in the Old Testament, we find a story about the whole world speaking the same common language.[30] The people pridefully built a city, ignoring God and focusing on their own strengths and abilities apart from him. They tried to build a tower that would enable them to ascend to the heavens without any sort of divine help. But God saw what they were doing and said, "If as one people speaking the same language they have begun to do this, then *nothing they plan to do will be impossible for them.* Come, let us go down and confuse their language so they will not understand each other."[31] God confused the people's language so they wouldn't do impossible things in their own strength. But now at Pentecost, God empowered the people to speak *known* languages because he had reestablished a people for whom nothing would be impossible.

---

[28] See Mark 16:15 and Matthew 28:19.
[29] See Luke 24:49 and Acts 1:4.
[30] See Genesis 11:1–9.
[31] Genesis 11:6–7, emphasis added.

Time is Short: When Paul wrote about speaking in tongues, he quoted the Old Testament prophet Isaiah and said that tongues were "a sign for unbelievers."[32] If we turn to the Old Testament and read Isaiah's words in context, we find God's promise to bring judgment. In Isaiah's prophecy, the sound of unknown tongues would be a sign to them that the promised judgment was coming quickly.[33]

Today, when Spirit-empowered Christians speak spontaneously in languages we don't know, we remember that the time is short. Jesus will soon return to bring judgment on the earth. He will destroy sin once and for all, but everyone living in that sin is in danger of being judged right along with it. The good news, however, is that he wants everyone to be saved. That's why the Father sent Jesus. And he has given us supernatural power to do impossible things (like minister healing and work miracles in his name) as we proclaim the wonderful message of his salvation to every nation, ethnicity, and people group around the world.[34]

You Can Be Baptized in the Holy Spirit

As a Christian who has put your faith in Jesus, you can be baptized in the Holy Spirit. Spirit baptism is not an achievement nor does it create any sort of elite class of Christian. James wrote that "God opposes the proud but gives grace to the humble."[35] If you want God to empower you, then a prideful pursuit of special spiritual status will have the

---

[32] See 1 Corinthians 14:21–22.
[33] See Isaiah 28:11–29.
[34] Much more could be said about "speaking in tongues," but this explanation specifically addresses some of the most likely reasons this strange expression of God's power on someone's life is given as a sign that a person has been baptized in the Holy Spirit.
[35] James 4:6.

opposite effect. God will oppose you. But if the desire of your heart is obedience, God will empower you.[36]

Your experience may not be quite like anyone else's. When the Holy Spirit came upon Jesus, he came like a dove.[37] When he came upon the disciples, he came like fire.[38] Some people have said they felt electricity. Others have said they felt an overwhelming peace. How the Holy Spirit makes himself known to you is less important than the fact that he is answering your prayer for power.

So set aside time to focus. Quiet yourself. Shut out distractions. Turn off your phone. Ask Jesus to baptize you in the Holy Spirit. And then, as soon as you become aware of the Holy Spirit's presence empowering you—no matter how he expresses himself to you—step out in faith to speak in tongues. Open your mouth and begin to speak in a language you don't know. Speak whatever sounds and syllables he inspires you to speak, and very quickly, you will find a new language pouring out of your mouth.

You can stop at any time. The Holy Spirit will not take over as though you're a puppet. He will simply fuel your speech as you yield to him.

This can happen for you right now where you are. But some people desire a more shared experience with someone praying for them. This, too, is biblical. If that's you, go to the person who gave you this book, or find another Spirit-filled believer whom you trust. You may want to have a pastor pray for you, but this isn't required. Simply know that if you want a pastor to pray for you to receive the baptism in the Holy

---

[36] See Acts 5:32.
[37] See Luke 3:21–22.
[38] See Acts 2:3.

ROOTED

Spirit, you'll need to find a Pentecostal or charismatic pastor.[39] No matter who it is, ask them to place their hands on you for the baptism in the Holy Spirit.[40]

Be Filled with the Holy Spirit

Lastly, after you're baptized in the Holy Spirit, an ongoing experience is available to you. The Bible calls it being "filled with the Holy Spirit." Whenever this happens in Scripture, people speak and act with great boldness.

Do not get drunk on wine, which leads to debauchery. Instead, be filled with the Spirit, speaking to one another with psalms, hymns, and songs from the Spirit. Sing and make music from your heart to the Lord, always giving thanks to God the Father for everything, in the name of our Lord Jesus Christ.[41]

While you can be filled with the Holy Spirit again and again, the goal for every believer is to live continually full of him. This happens only as we rely on God's presence and power—not only for a moment but for a lifetime.

Anytime you need a fresh filling from the Holy Spirit, turn your attention back to the Lord, ask to be filled, and wait until you sense the Lord answering your prayer.

With the Holy Spirit's help, you are ready to share the good news about Jesus with anyone you encounter. He will teach you and help you to fish for people.

---

[39] Not all Christians believe this biblical gift of the Holy Spirit's power is for today. Some churches even actively teach against it because it is foreign to their understanding and experience. I recommend finding an Assembly of God church or at least one that identifies as Spirit-filled.

[40] In Acts 8:14–17; 9:17; and 19:6, when someone who was baptized in the Holy Spirit placed their hands on someone else, that person received God's power too.

[41] Ephesians 5:18–20.

68

CHAPTER 6

SHARING YOUR HOPE

> *How, then, can they call on the one they have not*
> *believed in? And how can they believe in the one of whom*
> *they have not heard? And how can they hear*
> *without someone preaching to them?*
> *And how can anyone preach unless they are sent?*
> *As it is written: "How beautiful are the feet of*
> *those who bring good news!"*

—ROMANS 10:14–15

Toooot. This strange, mellow sound behind my head was a classmate in my college anthropology class, blowing across the mouth of a water bottle. Then his deep, resonant voice simply said, "Tugboat."

I couldn't contain my laughter. It was a strange enough action on its own, but the fact that he did this in the middle of a boring lecture—while our professor fumbled around with his computer, looking for photos of his trip to Samoa—instantly endeared me to the man. He was just the right amount of weird for me, and I thought, *I need to know this guy.*

During our break, I introduced myself. Jeff and I began hanging out after class each week. Early on, I asked him about his spiritual beliefs, and he told me he hadn't worked it all out, but he had mostly adopted a belief in Buddhism.

Naturally, this prompted questions about what I believed. Poor Jeff didn't know what he was getting into. Even though I had gone to church my whole life and had always loved Jesus, I had only recently understood God's power to transform my life. So with newfound zeal and a smile, I told Jeff my story about how God had changed my life, and I invited him to experience Jesus like I had.

Jeff wasn't interested in converting any time soon.

But we continued to laugh our way through that anthropology class and hang out during breaks and after lectures. I knew God was pursuing Jeff's heart, and I wanted to join my Father in his mission to reach this man.

Eventually, Jeff told me he had started attending a Wednesday night class at a church. As I asked him about it, I discovered God had led him to a class that my mentor in faith, Pastor Dan Vander Velde, was teaching. Jeff was coming to *my* church and didn't even realize it. Clearly, Jesus was working on Jeff, and I was merely helping.

At that time, the movie *The Passion* was in theaters. This R-rated depiction of Jesus's crucifixion, made by Mel Gibson, was shocking to many. It portrayed in detail the brutality Jesus endured for us. My church rented out an entire theater for people to attend for free, and I invited Jeff to come with me.

It wasn't the sort of movie you watch while eating popcorn. We left the theater in stunned silence.

Late that night, Jeff sat in my living room at my house. Moved in my heart by the Holy Spirit, I asked him, "After everything we've talked about over the last few months and after everything you saw tonight, is anything stopping you from giving your life to Jesus?"

Jeff admitted there wasn't.

"Then let's do this. I can pray with you right now, and you can become a follower of Jesus."

Jeff and I prayed together. That night, I enjoyed the incredible privilege and honor of leading my friend to salvation in Jesus. And Jesus gloriously saved him.

I immediately invited him to a weekly meeting that I led in the basement of my girlfriend's parents' house. Jeff came regularly, and God worked on his heart even more. He and I talked frequently on the phone. I answered his questions to the best of my ability. I probably said things incorrectly from time to time. I certainly wasn't perfect. But I kept pointing my friend toward a deeper relationship with Jesus.

And he kept going deeper with Jesus.

A few years later, Jeff felt God was leading him to study pastoral ministry, so he enrolled in classes at a local university that offered such a program. In time, he graduated, and soon, he helped another pastor I know start a new church in a nearby town.

Today, almost twenty years since I prayed with my friend in my living room, Jeff has a beautiful family. He still works a regular job that pays the bills, but he also regularly goes to parks and other places to tell people about Jesus. He and his family attend church and set a wonderful example of what it looks like to serve Jesus and his people.

You Can Do This Too

Way back in my anthropology class, I could have never guessed the number of people who have now been impacted by Jeff's obedience to Jesus. I was just a college student then myself. I was earning my degree in Early Childhood Development and Education. I wasn't a pastor or an expert on Christianity. I was just an ordinary guy who wanted all my friends to know Jesus like I did.

If God directs you to become a pastor or some other type of professional minister, great. But you don't have to do that to join Jesus in making disciples. You can be a college student like I was. Or you can be a childcare worker like I was after college. Or you can be a car salesman like my dad, who I told you about in chapter 4. Or you can be a security guard, like Jeff was for most of the last fifteen years. It really doesn't matter. If you follow Jesus with your whole heart, your faith will be contagious.

ROOTED

Get to Know the Good News

Peter, one of Jesus' followers, wrote the following advice:

> But in your hearts revere Christ as Lord. Always be prepared to give an answer to everyone who asks you to give the reason for the hope that you have. But do this with gentleness and respect, keeping a clear conscience, so that those who speak maliciously against your good behavior in Christ may be ashamed of their slander.[1]

If you don't yet feel prepared to give someone a reason for why you have such hope in Jesus, I believe what I'm about to share will change your views. Notice also that Peter took time to emphasize *how* we should share our hope with people—"with gentleness and respect, keeping a clear conscience." You don't have to act like a know-it-all to introduce people to Jesus. In fact, you don't even have to know all that much.

The Bible is big. Even after studying it my whole life, I still understand some parts better than others. I find some parts strange or confusing. I still have questions about some passages. Clearly, my effectiveness for Jesus is not based on how much I know.

To be fair, I do read voraciously and have accumulated a great deal of knowledge over the years. But I started doing wild things for Jesus back when I knew very little.

The word "gospel" means "good news." We typically use this term to refer to the message about Jesus. You may remember that the Bible books of Matthew, Mark, Luke, and John, which each tell the story of Jesus's life, death, and resurrection, are called the four Gospels.

---

[1] 1 Peter 3:15–16.

But the gospel is much bigger than what is contained in those four books. The good news about Jesus stretches all the way back before the universe was created. John even started his Gospel by saying of Jesus, "Through him all things were made; without him nothing was made that has been made."[2] Jesus was present and active, along with the Father and the Holy Spirit, at the time of creation.

Speaking metaphorically about Jesus and his sacrifice to set us free from sin, the Scriptures call Jesus "the Lamb who was slain from the creation of the world."[3] In other words, the decision had already been made. Jesus was prepared and determined even then to go to the cross and set us free from sin. God preemptively met the consequences for our sin, even before the first sin was committed. His plan was always redemption.

But the gospel doesn't just stretch into the past. It also stretches into the future. Paul wrote, "The gospel is bearing fruit and growing throughout the whole world—just as it has been doing among you since the day you heard it and truly understood God's grace."[4]

How does the gospel grow? The good news about Jesus not only includes the story of all the wonderful things he did when he walked this earth. It not only contains the story of all he did throughout the Old Testament in concert with the Father and the Spirit. The good news about Jesus includes the story of everything Jesus has continued to do right up to this moment.

If you think about it, there's no such thing as a complete gospel presentation. Even the Bible, as wonderful and helpful as it is, does not contain the last two thousand years of good news about Jesus. The Bible doesn't even contain all the good

---

[2] John 1:3.
[3] Revelation 13:8.
[4] Colossians 1:6.

news about what Jesus did when he walked this earth.[5] The gospel is still growing all over the world, and those stories need to be told too.

Part of the gospel is what Jesus did to save and transform me. In fact, as you read my story about Jeff, you read another part of this growing gospel, seeing the good things Jesus did for my friend.

You are reading this book because your life is now part of the gospel. Jesus is working in your life, and that's good news. You have a testimony to share about your own personal experiences with Jesus.

And here's the best part: You are the foremost expert in the world on your personal piece of the gospel. No one knows your piece of Jesus's story better than you do. That means you have a responsibility to glorify Jesus by sharing your piece of his story with anyone you can.

I know you're fairly new to this whole idea of following Jesus. But you don't have to know all the stories in the Bible to share your testimony. You know that Jesus died and rose again. And you know what that has meant for your own life. Tell those things to the people you know, and the gospel will continue to grow through you.

Sharing Your Story

Your story about Jesus is a powerful weapon that conquers the devil himself.[6] The key is making sure Jesus shines more brightly in your story than anyone else. This doesn't require you to embellish anything; it simply requires you to be truthful. No matter how much of a role you played in making good decisions or obeying God and no matter how

---

[5] See John 21:25.
[6] See Revelation 12:11.

wonderful the person was who reached you, Jesus still did the heavy lifting. He alone is your Savior.

One of the best ways to ensure that Jesus shines as you share your story is to include the message about his life, death, and resurrection. In chapter 1, I shared my own personal testimony and wove into it the truth I learned about how I have died with Jesus and received new life from his Spirit. You can talk about how the message was explained to you or how you came to understand that when Jesus died, your sin died, and now God has made you a new creation. Explain what that means.

Generally speaking, our personal salvation testimony consists of three parts: (1) who I once was, (2) how Jesus reached me, and (3) what is different about my life now.

For example, I was once abused, depressed, and addicted. I wanted freedom but wasn't strong enough to live differently for more than a couple of weeks. But God reached me as I was reading the sixth chapter of Romans in the Bible. He showed me that I could consider myself dead because somehow, I died when Jesus died. Then Jesus raised from the dead, and the same Spirit of God who raised Jesus from the dead came to live inside me and make me a completely new person. Today, I'm free from the mess of my old life. I have a relationship with God, I experience miracles, and my heart has been changed so that I truly love people.

It's that simple. I took those three points and wrote two or three sentences for each. That little paragraph isn't my whole story, but it is accurate.

Learn to tell your story concisely, as I just did, so you can rattle it off in under one minute. The shorter, the better. You can always add more details when telling your story to someone, but it's hard to intentionally leave out details in the middle of a conversation. For this reason, I recommend practicing—even memorizing—a short version like the one I just shared. That way, when you're in the middle of sharing your story, you don't have to think about what details to omit.

ROOTED

Instead, you can focus on what details to include that would most benefit the person to whom you're talking.

A Life Lived for Jesus Is Contagious

In this present-day piece of the gospel, you'll see how a life lived for Jesus—coupled with telling people what Jesus has done in your life—will spread the good news about Jesus to others.

One of my closest friends throughout the last ten years has been James Loruss. Together, we've preached about Jesus all over the world, written books, made movies, and more. But in the very beginning, James was just a college student who came to the meetings I held in my house. He often stayed afterward—sometimes late into the night (or rather, the next morning)—asking questions about God and seeking my advice.

After I took my first trip to Uganda in October 2011, James asked me how it went. I answered, "It was amazing. And next time, I'm taking you with me."

In June 2012, James and I visited Uganda together. We saw countless miracles as God healed people and gave them real freedom through Jesus.

When we returned, James and I hosted a special testimony night. We invited everyone who had donated money for our trip. We fed them a Ugandan meal, told stories, and showed videos we had taken there.

James invited his older brother, Joe. At the time, Joe wasn't following Jesus. He had grown up attending church, but he was living for himself. Nevertheless, since his brother invited him, Joe came to the meeting.

As Joe watched video after video of miracles and listened to testimony after testimony of what God did on our short trip, he became sharply aware of the aimlessness of his own life. Joe's heart was stirred as we proclaimed the good news about what Jesus had done in Uganda. Throughout the night, he sat further and further forward in his seat, going from slouching with his arms folded to leaning forward on his elbows. After the meeting, he asked his little brother James, "So this is really serious for you, isn't it?"

Something awakened in Joe that night. A few weeks later, he too started attending the meetings I held in my house. His life began to transform. His marriage began to transform. In February 2014, Joe came with us to Uganda and led a construction team who helped build the first structure of the orphanage I've started there. He has returned with me multiple times over the years.

Meanwhile, Joe has worked full time building houses. And at the same time, he intentionally invests his life in mentoring others. Today, he is on the board of my nonprofit, helping me manage the orphanage project in Uganda. He's also on the staff of my church and leads a group of about twenty people in his home every week. He's leading people to salvation, baptizing them, and helping them learn to follow Jesus.

In so many ways, Joe is an ordinary guy who likes working with his hands, hunting, and having fun with his family. He balances his work and family life beautifully. And along with that, he shines brightly for Jesus wherever he goes and looks for opportunities to bring others closer to God.

Anybody can do this. If you are a follower of Jesus, empowered by his Holy Spirit, anything is possible. You can introduce your friends to Jesus, and they can go on to introduce others to him. This is how God's story grows. This is how God's family grows.

Joe can do it.

James can do it.

Jeff can do it.

I can do it.

You can do it.

ROOTED

CHAPTER 7:
STRENGTH TO ENDURE

But we do not belong to those who shrink back and are destroyed,
but to those who have faith and are saved.

—HEBREWS 10:39

The African sun was hot, but the banana trees provided a
pleasant shade. We were seated outside on thick, upholstered
foam that cushioned handmade wooden furniture, overlooking
a vast field of soybeans, cassava, and groundnuts. Our host—a
village elder—whispered in his servant's ear. Soon a short
wooden table was placed in front of us, and platters of fruit,
rice, chicken, beans, and more were added. It was a feast fit for
a king, and this well-off leader wanted to honor us for visiting
his home.

Pastor Paul, who brought me here at the old man's
request, leaned over to me and said, "When I first came to this
village thirteen years ago, I was beaten by this man's sons in
this very place, under this same banana tree."

At that time, Paul had led one of this man's two wives to
salvation in Jesus. Her sons were furious that the new pastor in
the village had "corrupted" their mother. When they next saw
him, they dragged him there beneath the banana tree and beat
him severely, hoping to persuade him to leave their village.

But Paul continued to faithfully serve the people of
Wanenga. He refused to give up, and God strengthened him

to endure the many attacks and persecution. In time, the old man's sons became Christians too, and later, so did he.

As I sat there with Pastor Paul, thirteen years later, the village had become primarily Christian because of his labor for Jesus. The feast before us represented far more than an old man's wealth or the hard work of his hired servants. It represented my friend's bruised and bloodied body, his agonizing prayers, and his courageous love for the people of that village. Never has a meal moved my heart like the one I ate that day.

Empowered Endurance

Around the year AD 160, a Christian known as Justin Martyr wrote, "Now it is evident that no one can terrify or subdue us who have believed in Jesus over all the world. For it is plain that, though beheaded, and crucified, and thrown to wild beasts, and chains, and fire, and all other kinds of torture, we do not give up our confession; but the more such things happen, the more do others and in larger numbers become faithful, and worshippers of God through the name of Jesus."[1]

The early Christians lived in a world where their beliefs cost them their safety and often even their lives. Today, many around the world live the same way.

Recently, I was driving in my car and praying. Out of the corner of my eye, I noticed an American flag blowing in the wind. It prompted me to pray, "Lord, thank you for the privilege of living in a country where I have the freedom to worship you and speak freely about you so that I can make a bigger impact than I would be able to in many other nations."

---

[1] Justin Martyr, Alexander Roberts, ed., "Dialogue with Trypho, Chapter CX." *The Ante-Nicene Fathers: The Apostolic Fathers, Justin Martyr, Irenaeus, Volume 1*, (Peabody, Massachusetts: Hendrickson Publishers, 2004), 254.

Immediately, the Lord corrected me. Images flashed through my mind of secret churches in China, passionate Christians in African villages where persecution is common, Indian believers who continue to spread their faith even after their homes have been burned, and more. The Holy Spirit spoke to me in my thoughts and said, "Your effectiveness does not come from your country. It comes from me. You are effective because I have called you. You would make just as much of an impact in a restricted nation as you make here. Your country does not empower your ministry—I do."

I immediately repented. And then I sensed God's love for me. I recognized that he gives grace to those who need it. You may feel right now as though you could never endure what other Christians have endured. But the grace to endure a beating is only given to a Christian who is being beaten. The grace to endure the confiscation of one's property is only given to the one whose property is being taken. You don't need to worry about all the what-ifs. You can rest, simply knowing that no matter what comes your way, God will give you supernatural grace that will help you rise above that challenge.

After promising his followers that they would be persecuted and scattered, Jesus said, "I have told you these things, so that in me you may have peace. In this world you will have trouble. But take heart! I have overcome the world."[2]

When we hear these words, we often think about how Jesus overcame the world through his death and resurrection. But when Jesus spoke these words, he hadn't yet gone to the cross. Jesus was talking about something else. He had faced temptation, opposition, insults, slander, and more. In all these things, he consistently overcame.

Persecution is inevitable. The Bible promises, "In fact, everyone who wants to live a godly life in Christ Jesus will be

---

[2] John 16:33.

persecuted."[3] But the one who consistently overcame the
world lives in us. The one who always beat temptation lives in
us. The one who stood up under extreme social pressure lives
in us. The one who endured the cross lives in us. If we will
consider ourselves dead and trust him to express that
passionate perseverance through us, he will. Apart from him,
we'll fail.[4] In the words of Jesus, "With man this is impossible,
but with God all things are possible."[5]

The persecution you and I experience may never rise to
the level that my friends, like Paul, have endured. Perhaps we
will only face insults or rejection. Perhaps people will try to
intimidate or mock us. Whatever the case, persecution is
inevitable, but Jesus has already proven his strength to endure
it. You can rest in that truth.

It's Not about Being Nice

Too often in my country, people assume that the
Christian life is just about becoming a nicer person—someone
who lives in a way that might make others wonder why we're
so kindhearted and sweet.

My friends overseas are nice too. Some of them are the
most hospitable and sweet-natured people I've ever met. Why,
then, would people attack them? Why would their families and
neighbors persecute them for being such decent people?

The answer is simple: That's not why they're persecuted.

No one really cares whether you're nice. They care
about their own lives. They take notice when the morality of
your life exposes their wickedness. They are upset when your
message confronts their selfish desires. They lash out when
your lifestyle threatens their self-justified consciences.
Suddenly, you become an enemy because your presence

---

[3] 2 Timothy 3:12.
[4] See John 15:5.
[5] Matthew 19:36.

makes that person feel like their entire way of life is in jeopardy.

And it is.

The Christian life is more than niceness. It's a lifestyle that invites people to die. We do this through the message we share, the attitudes we show, and the actions we take. With boldness from the Holy Spirit, we refuse to be quiet about our faith. We offer to pray for people. We expect miracles to happen as God answers those prayers. And we introduce people to the God we serve.

In some places around the world, that sort of lifestyle will lead to being beaten under a banana tree. In some places, it's a fast road to death by martyrdom. In other places, it's a reason to be fired from your job, rejected by your friends, or teased by your family. But no matter where you live, persecution is inevitable. For this reason, if you're not experiencing some form of persecution, you may need to be a little bolder with your love, kindness, and message. Don't worry about the cost; Jesus is worth it.

You Can't Scare a Dead Man

You can't threaten a dead person with death. They're already dead. The Christian life has no room for self-preservation because the whole point is to crucify the self-life and rise up in the power of a life united with Jesus. We no longer live for ourselves. We live for the one who saved us from sin and united us with our heavenly Father.

A friend of mine named Tom worked at a printing company, operating the large commercial press. After some time working there, the company took a job printing a swimsuit calendar. But Tom refused to pull the lever on his machine, saying he was opposed to the objectification of women and couldn't do the work with a clear conscience. He was given the option of doing the job or being fired, and he decided to stand his ground and surrender his job.

ROOTED

The next few years weren't easy for Tom. I wish I could tell you that God worked an immediate miracle that made it all worth the price he paid. But what makes an act like this worth the cost is not some miracle—it's Jesus. He's worth it.

Today, Tom is in a much better situation, but it didn't come without great challenges to him and his family. Nevertheless, he did what he knew was right. God's grace sustained him and empowered him to follow through. And I know a reward is waiting for Tom in heaven.

This is the lifestyle that invites persecution, and that makes it the lifestyle that God empowers. God doesn't need to empower those who don't need him. The army doesn't hand its best weapons to cowards running away from the battle. It hands them to those resolved to go to the frontlines. Likewise, the Holy Spirit gives supernatural abilities only as he determines in his wisdom that we will need such tools.[6]

God is looking for dead people. He's looking for those who aren't striving to maintain their present lives. He's looking for people who have chosen to disregard the status quo and follow him no matter the cost.

In the previous chapter, I taught you how to share your personal story with someone, and I told you that it's a powerful weapon that conquers the devil himself. But there's a little more to it than that. John prophesied,

> They triumphed over [Satan]
>   by the blood of the Lamb
>   and by the word of their testimony;
> they did not love their lives so much
>   as to shrink from death.[7]

---

[6] 1 Corinthians 12:11.
[7] Revelation 12:11.

The "blood of the Lamb" refers to the self-sacrificial blood of Jesus that was shed on the cross for us. The "word of their testimony" is our declaration of how Jesus's death and resurrection have affected our lives. But a third thing here overcomes the devil: We do not love our lives so much that we cower in the face of death. In other words, we share our story and the message of Jesus no matter the consequences.

Eternal Life

One of the most famous passages of Scripture is John 3:16: "For God so loved the world that he gave his one and only Son, that whoever believes in him shall not perish but have eternal life."

Many Christians talk about eternal life as something that happens after you die. That's sort of true, but I died with Christ a long time ago. Eternal life isn't something I look forward to; it's something I have.

Jesus prayed, "Now this is eternal life: that they know you, the only true God, and Jesus Christ, whom you have sent."[8] Eternal life starts now, not later.

Because I have eternal life, I no longer count the days since I last sinned. I no longer self-analyze whether I'm worthy to partner with God based on how well I've performed—whether I've read enough of my Bible or prayed long enough. I simply rest in my relationship with God and live in the moment. To know him is to have eternal life.

When you understand the eternal life we've been given, your priorities shift from temporary ones to eternal. You start investing your life more in things that will last (like the souls of other people) rather than things that will perish (like wealth or earthly prestige).

Jesus taught his followers to focus on what matters.

---

[8] John 17:3.

Do not store up for yourselves treasures on earth, where moths and vermin destroy, and where thieves break in and steal. But store up for yourselves treasures in heaven, where moths and vermin do not destroy, and where thieves do not break in and steal. For where your treasure is, there your heart will be also ....

Therefore I tell you, do not worry about your life, what you will eat or drink; or about your body, what you will wear. Is not life more than food, and the body more than clothes? Look at the birds of the air; they do not sow or reap or store away in barns, and yet your heavenly Father feeds them. Are you not much more valuable than they? Can any one of you by worrying add a single hour to your life?

And why do you worry about clothes? See how the flowers of the field grow. They do not labor or spin. Yet I tell you that not even Solomon in all his splendor was dressed like one of these. If that is how God clothes the grass of the field, which is here today and tomorrow is thrown into the fire, will he not much more clothe you—you of little faith? So do not worry, saying, 'What shall we eat?' or 'What shall we drink?' or 'What shall we wear?' For the pagans run after all these things, and your heavenly Father knows that you need them. But seek first his kingdom and his righteousness, and all these things will be given to you as well. Therefore do not worry about tomorrow, for tomorrow will worry about itself. Each day has enough trouble of its own.[9]

We are all invited to live with absolute trust in the Father's love for us. When our mind is set on heavenly things, earthly things matter less. We're still allowed to enjoy

---

[9] Matthew 6:19–21, 25–34.

whatever earthly things God has given us.[10] But our attention is no longer on how to accumulate those things[11] but instead fixed on Jesus—the one who endured the cross without concern for the shame or humiliation of the process.[12] And as the gaze of our hearts remains settled on him, we find ourselves becoming more like him.

As Paul wrote, "And we all, who ... contemplate the Lord's glory, are being transformed into his image with ever-increasing glory, which comes from the Lord, who is the Spirit."[13] Other translations render the word "contemplate" as "behold." The more clearly we can perceive Jesus, the more fully we become like him. And one day, we will see him in his fullness and become like him in his fullness. As John wrote, "See what great love the Father has lavished on us, that we should be called children of God! And that is what we are! The reason the world does not know us is that it did not know him. Dear friends, now we are children of God, and what we will be has not yet been made known. But we know that when Christ appears, we shall be like him, for we shall see him as he is."[14]

Whenever you're not sure what to do, focus on Jesus. You'll become more like him as he expresses his life through you. Whenever you find yourself in a challenge or trial that feels too big for you, focus on Jesus. The one who has already overcome the world will overcome through you. Whenever persecution arises, focus on Jesus. The one who endured the cross will endure through you.

Nothing is too difficult for Jesus, and he lives in you. You know him, and you have eternal life.

---

[10] See 1 Timothy 6:17.
[11] See 1 Timothy 6:6–10.
[12] Hebrews 12:1–3.
[13] 2 Corinthians 3:18.
[14] 1 John 3:1–2.

87

ROOTED

Complete Surrender

Here in the United States, we have a cultural aversion to the word "surrender." But in the times of the Bible, surrender could mean being assimilated into a superior nation with a superior economy, a superior military, superior technology, superior infrastructure, and more. Rather than defeat, sometimes surrender was a significant upgrade.

My friends David and Paula answered Jesus's invitation to fish for people. They wanted to help the vulnerable to become disciples of Jesus. So they connected with a local extension of the global ministry Teen Challenge. As men who entered the Christian rehab program graduated, David befriended them and helped them grow in their faith.

David, Paula, and their four children moved out of their own home and into David's parents' home. Why? Because they wanted to offer up their own house for three or four of these men to live. Every week, they hold church services, prayer meetings, and Bible studies in that house. David helps them find work and mentors them in their new lifestyles.

I know another couple that surrendered their home because the husband's brother and sister-in-law (in another state) were out of work and on the brink of homelessness with their children. That move saved their family and enabled them to start thriving.

My friends Jon and Heather gave their car away, not knowing where they would find another vehicle, and God provided them with a better one the very next day, for free.

My friend Paul in Uganda has shown me what it looks like to persevere in the strength of the Holy Spirit. He moved away from the city into a village where he knew he would be persecuted. And there he has lived for over two decades with his wife, five children, an old man named John, and dozens of orphans who are now sons and daughters of God.

We can't all give away our houses and cars, but friends like mine remind us that a life surrendered to Jesus is the best life possible. When we surrender to him, we enter a new and superior kingdom.

As I said at the beginning of chapter 1, Christianity is the most thrilling, difficult, fun, risky, comforting, scary, fulfilling, and life-transforming lifestyle in existence. It's full of both blessings and challenges. There are mountaintops so high you'll think you're already in heaven, and there are valleys so low you might wonder if you made the right choice.

But I wouldn't trade it for anything.

Jesus is worth any cost.

And he loves you more than you could ever imagine.

ROOTED

ROOTSCHURCH

ONE MISSION. ONE FAMILY. MANY HOMES.

Roots Church is a Spirit-filled network of house churches. That means our church meetings happen in small groups that gather in people's homes (rather than in a traditional building).

Since you're now part of God's family, we're already connected, but we would love to grow in a meaningful relationship with you. The person who gave you this book would be happy to bring you to the church they attend, whether it's with us here at Roots or at another church near you.

If you join us at Roots, we'll meet in someone's home, discuss the Bible, pray for each other, sing, and share stories of what God is doing in our lives. Feel free to watch quietly or dive right into the discussion, whichever you prefer. Some of our churches share meals, and others have snacks. All of our churches love Jesus and desire to know him more. Come as you are, and there's no need to bring anything except your own eagerness to grow in faith and love.

www.RootsAG.org

CONTACT INFO

The person who gave you this book would love to hear from you, answer any questions, and help you thrive in your new life in Christ.

Christianity is best experienced in the context of friendships and healthy community. This person would be happy to have some one-on-one conversations with you, and as soon as you're ready, they'd love to introduce you to their church.

Feel free to reach out today.

Name:

Phone / Email:

Made in USA - Kendallville, IN
27279_9780998817187
06.18.2022 1314